D1365452

TREATING AND EVALUATING
THE WARRIORS OF THE NFL

PLAYING HURT

TREATING AND EVALUATING THE WARRIORS OF THE NFL

PLAYING HURT

PIERCE E. SCRANTON, JR., M.D.

Foreword by Tom Flores

BRASSEY'S, INC.
Washington, D.C.

Library of Congress Cataloging-in-Publication Data

Scranton, Pierce E.

    Playing hurt : treating and evaluating the warriors of the NFL / Pierce E. Scranton, Jr.; foreword by Tom Flores.—1st ed.

      p. cm.

    Includes index.

    ISBN 1-57488-397-6 (alk. paper)

    1. Scranton, Pierce E. 2. Sports physicians—Washington (State)—Seattle—Biography. 3. Seattle Seahawks (Football team) 4. Football injuries—Washington (State)—Seattle. I. Title.

RC1220.F6 S376 2001

617.1′027′092—dc21

[B]

                                  2001037859

Printed in the United States of America on acid-free paper that meets the American National Standards Institute Z39-48 Standard.

Brassey's, Inc.

22841 Quicksilver Drive

Dulles, Virginia 20166

First Edition

10 9 8 7 6 5 4 3 2 1

CONTENTS

FOREWORD

by Tom Flores

I've spent almost my entire life in amateur, organized, and professional football. I attended the College of the Pacific (University of the Pacific) in Stockton, California. After graduation, I had brief tryouts with the Calgary Stampeders and the Washington Redskins, but I was hampered by a shoulder injury which had occurred in college and required surgery. It took longer to heal than I expected. Eventually I found a home in 1960 with the Oakland Raiders in the American Football League. I was a quarterback with the Raiders for six years, then went on to the Buffalo Bills for two years. My final two seasons were spent with the Kansas City Chiefs, during which time we won Super Bowl IV.

Of my 35 years in professional football, I was an active player for 10 seasons. In 1971, I began my professional coaching career with the Buffalo Bills. I then returned to the Raiders as an assistant coach in 1972, and in 1976, we were crowned champions in Super Bowl IX. In 1979, I became head coach of the Raiders, a position I held for nine years. During that time, I led the team to world crowns in Super Bowls XV and XVIII. I retired from active coaching in 1988, though I stayed on as a consultant. The next year, Ken Behring hired me to be the president and general manager of the Seattle Seahawks, and I became head coach and general manager in 1992.

With my background as a player, assistant coach, head coach, and general manager, I've witnessed and been a part of the evolution of medicine in professional sports, and I feel highly qualified to comment on team physicians and their importance in America's number-one sport. In 1959, I had surgery on my right shoulder. Drs. Lucky and Clark in Stockton, California, per-formed the operation. At that time, the surgery was regarded as a new exploratory operation. Rehabilitation took more than a year. Today, I'm sure that same operation could be done quite quickly. My second shoulder operation was performed by Dr. Joe Godfrey of the Buffalo Bills. I'd suffered a freak injury, a ruptured pectoralis major muscle. Back then, the diagnosis was difficult, but with today's MRIs, I'm sure it would be easy.

When I came to Seattle, I tore the cartilage in my knee, and Dr. Pierce Scranton performed the surgery in 1989. I was able to walk right out of the hospital and resume my normal duties as president/general manager without any down time. In 1994 and 1995, I tore my right rotator cuff and then my left. Drs. Scranton and Auld, the two team physicians for the Seattle Seahawks, performed the surgery. In all of my surgeries, I was fortunate to have doctors whom I trusted and respected.

During my years in the NFL as a head coach and general manager, I always had a close relationship with our doctors. I felt it was necessary to get to know each one, not only as a doctor, but as a person. It was important to me that our team doctors have strong feelings about our team's health and loyalty to the entire organization. When our doctors came into the training room, I didn't want the feeling that outsiders were invading us. They had to feel part of the family, and we had to treat them as such.

When I joined the Seahawk organization, I didn't know Dr. Scranton, but we became acquainted very soon after my arrival. The thing that stood out most about Dr. Scranton was his ability to express his professional expertise in a very relaxed fashion. He did not treat people as just numbers. He referred to every player or employee with warmth and sincerity. If he had a fault, it might well have been that he was too sensitive. It's a tough task when you care deeply about your patients, because not every person is fortunate enough to recover fully.

I believe doctors like Pierce Scranton are the unsung heroes in the world of professional sports. When they succeed, as he often did, it's expected; when they fail, they're chastised by the misinformed. A doctor such as Pierce does not become a team physician for monetary gain. I know because I negotiated his fee. He takes on the challenge for the love of the game and the satisfaction of making and keeping players healthy. His personal commitment and professionalism were the best, and he always did his job with class.

Tom Flores
Indian Wells, California

INTRODUCTION

Major League Baseball likes to bill itself as "America's Pastime," but if you really want to look into the heart and soul of this country, drive through any small town in America on a crisp fall Friday night and look for the lights. Look for the stadium's glare illuminating the cobalt autumn sky. Listen carefully and you'll hear the band, the roar of a crowd; maybe you'll catch the scent of booster-club hot dogs sizzling on a barbecue. This is American football, a microcosm that reflects the psyche, social foundation, and soul of communities across this nation.

Come closer and immerse yourself in the lights and sounds. Under the bleachers, rug rats chase each other, laughing as they play, swinging and climbing from the braces. They scuffle in the leaves, looking for dropped change. Above them a roar erupts into the night. The crowd, cheerleaders, and band follow the looping aerial arc of a spinning pigskin ball hurtled downfield by a skinny kid who will escort the homecoming queen at halftime. He has just learned to shave. Streaking under the ball's arc, legs churning and neck bobbing beneath a beat-up Riddell helmet, is another kid. He leaps and improbably snatches the ball from the air, clutching it to his chest. Touchdown! Thunder rumbles through the bleachers as the crowd rises to its feet, clapping and cheering. An avalanche of loose change clatters under the stands. The rug rats go wild. All the while, the band blares the school fight song.

These are the roots of American sports. However, from these laudable roots have grown many convoluted and twisted branches. Like the Friday night high-school contests, *Monday Night Football* has become a ritual in America. One game in particular stands out in my mind. It was November 1997, and the Kansas City Chiefs were playing the Denver Broncos. The Chiefs' tight end ran a crossing route and extended his arms to catch an Elvis Grbac pass. As he caught the ball, he was tackled from behind. His knees hit the ground. His arms were still outstretched, and his head was unprotected. He was speared helmet to helmet by a crossing defensive back. The force of this blow snapped his head and body backwards, causing his feet to flip up off the ground as his helmet and torso jackknifed and slammed into the turf. This collision was replayed in slow motion from many different angles, the translation of violent kinetics into unconsciousness. Announcer Frank Gifford lamely reassured us that the motionless tight end had been downed by a "completely legitimate" blow. Eventually, after three commercial breaks, the medical staff carted the player off on a backboard, his head safety-strapped and immobile.

A few series later, the Denver defensive end did an inside stunt, and Grbac was pile-driven into the turf. His clavicle snapped as three hundred pounds of rushing defensive lineman crushed his shoulder into the ground. There were more reverse angle and slow-motion shots of this event. This time, Gifford commented that the referee's penalty flag for intentional grounding was entirely appropriate, because Elvis never got out of the pocket. ABC stalled for time with more commercial breaks as the Kansas City medical staff tried to get Grbac, who was writhing in agony, off the field. I wound up switching off the television. I wondered how the doctors were going to react to this dilemma. I was sure that Elvis was in good hands, because I've known the Kansas City doctors, Jon Browne and his partner, Chris Barnehouse, for over a decade, and they're two of the finer doctors in the league. After 17 years in the NFL, though, I was glad I would no longer have to deal with the problems Jon would be facing. For example, did the unconscious tight end suffer a concussion, a broken neck, a spinal cord injury, a skull fracture—or all of the above? A severe concussion alone will undoubtedly trigger a three-ring circus. There will be questions from the player's family, his agent, the coaches, and management. A host of quasi-medical wannabes will publicly offer quack remedies and free "special" treatments such as herbs, potions, magnets, and crystals. Dr. Browne will have to decide if and when this tight end can play again—assuming the injury was "only" a concussion. If Dr. Browne decides to play it safe and hold him out of the next game, he might feel subtle pressure from the player, his team, the player's agent, the coaches, and management. *Why isn't he playing? Hey, doc, how's our boy?* If the doctor risks letting him play, and the tight end suffers another concussion or a "second-impact syndrome" that causes permanent brain damage, he will be vilified in the press, accused of being a spineless tool of management, a mere puppet unwilling to protect the health and safety of the player.

I know that in the end, Jon will seek out the best expert advice available, listen patiently, and finally use his own good judgment to make what he believes to be the best decision. In trying to provide prudent medical care for those who inflict and suffer violence as sport, Jon is caught between a rock and a hard place. He has to decide every day whether it is okay for players to play hurt, or to play hurt shot up with painkillers, or whether it's not okay. The main difficulty in these decisions is that the incentives for the player to play with pain are huge: a game-day check, more money than many Americans earn in a year. The stakes are high for the team, too. An entire coaching staff could be fired because the loss of a talented player can lead to losses on the field. The doctor is caught in the middle, forced to distinguish between the usual aches and pains of football versus the pain of an injury that could make that player more vulnerable to serious harm.

I stared at the blank TV screen. There has been an incredible evolution in the way medical decisions in the NFL are made, but no one has recorded it. For 17 years, I've made some of those decisions myself. Now I've decided to tell you what it's been like, spending almost two decades in the NFL, on the sidelines, in the draft-day "war room," in the playoffs, on Commissioner Paul Tagliabue's NFL Safety Committee, and in a court of law. I've decided to lift the veil of secrecy and give you a peek behind the scenes.

Early on, some of the publishing houses reviewing this project wanted me to juice up the story. They wanted me to emphasize unethical teams and the sleazy doctors who are tools of management, maybe even dig up some player or agent scandals, too. Then, as the work progressed, Seahawk management got wind of the book and wanted to "review" it before publication. Juicing up the story might sell books, but it would cheapen the richness of my NFL experiences. And notwithstanding the public relations concerns of the Seahawks and the NFL, I've decided to exercise my First Amendment rights and give you an unabridged account of my medical experience in the League.

I'm going to take you through a typical year in the NFL from a medical perspective. This is too big a job for me to do by myself, so I've enlisted some help. Tom Flores was a player, coach, head coach, president, and general manager in the NFL. He's one of the few people in the world who owns four different Super Bowl rings from his career as a player and coach. He's here to give you his thoughts on medicine from the perspectives of both a player and a team official. Jack Mills, one of the best agents in the NFL for more than 31 years, will also share his views. Finally, I'm going to get a little help from the best: a Hall-of-Fame trainer, Jimmy Whitesel, and players such as former All-Pro running back Curt Warner, safety Paul Moyer, and others. They'll tell you what it's like to play hurt, to taste victory, and to come back from catastrophic injury.

ONE

The Winter Meat Market:
Combine Physicals

In Indianapolis in February, it gets dark early, and it's cold as hell. Icy gusts swirl through the streets, catching paper cups, newspapers, and the hats of the unwary in a spiraling curtain of snow. Each winter, Jimmy Whitesel and I visited this freezing environment. Jimmy was the head trainer for the Seattle Seahawks. We'd gingerly pick our way down Illinois Street, tiptoeing through dirty piles of frozen slush towards St. Elmo Steak House. Jimmy had been a trainer with the Seahawks from the beginning, since the franchise was founded in 1976. Picture a guy who looks a little like Buddy Hackett, maybe throw in just a touch of Opus from the old *Bloom County* comics, add a heart of gold, and you'll come close to Jimmy. He's everything you could ask for in a trainer: mother hen, father confessor, your best friend, and dad to a fine family. He's one of the all-time greatest, now in the Trainer Hall of Fame. Jimmy is largely responsible for the successful return of many an injured athlete. In 1989, he was voted NFL Trainer of the Year, the best in the country. He deserved it.

So why did we endure Indy's freezing climatic abuse? For the NFL combine physicals. Every February, all 28 (now 31) NFL teams "combined" to send their scouts, coaches, and medical staff to a geographically central location to physically examine the college players eligible for the upcoming draft. These combine exams were first held in Phoenix, then New Orleans, and now, for the past decade, in Indianapolis.

In earlier years, combine physicals as we now know them didn't exist. There was a scouting grapevine. Team scouts traveled by train, bus, and rental car, looking up old friends in the college-football world, asking them who was good and who might be a sleeper. They carried a pocket full of

1

dimes and quarters for long-distance calls. Were the talented players they'd identified really that talented? Big-name college seniors were shuffled from city to city at the whim of interested teams. As draft day approached, these players were on the road, not in school where they belonged. The process was time-consuming and sometimes no more accurate at assessing talent than a roll of the dice. For many teams, draft day meant "craps out." In the 1960s, the rival NFL and AFL merged to form today's NFL. The teams therefore decided to pool their efforts into larger scouting groups. There was a 13-team Tampa Bay combine and a 10-team Detroit combine. The Seattle Seahawks, Buffalo Bills, San Francisco 49ers, and Dallas Cowboys banded together to form their own mini-combine. The Raiders stayed on their own until Commissioner Pete Rozelle forced them to join our four-team combine.

The combines cut down on the teams' overlap of travel and testing. Even so, the NCAA wasn't happy about the frequent travel by student athletes prior to the draft. A single combine physical was the logical end result. But don't assume that a single combine means a potential draft choice gets only one exam. Not on your life! No team trusts some other team's doctor or scouts to determine a player's suitability. So, for one whole day, any player who sets foot in Indianapolis will be poked, prodded, twisted, yanked, ascultated, percussed, and have his limbs pulled on by all 31 team orthopedists, all 31 team internists, and all the scouts as well.

So that's why Jimmy and I would go to Indianapolis. On our first night, we always eat at the same restaurant. Jimmy's made reservations, and we shoulder our way past a shivering crowd lined up outside the door. We ignore their grumbling and push through the dark-stained, double-foyer doors that seal St. Elmo Steak House from the cold. Jimmy stops to sniff and blow his Opus-like appendage. A sign at the entrance proclaims St. Elmo "Famous Since 1902." We pass rows of glass cases that display expensive California cabernets and French Bordeaux wines. Next is a selection of fine, hand-rolled Honduran and Dominican cigars: Macanudos, Santa Rosas, and Partagas. Finally, we eye the thick slabs of carefully aged, red marbled meat. We're starving, and I think, maybe one of each? A tuxedoed maitre d' ushers us down the hall past walls of signed photographs of sports celebrities, movie stars, and oversize photos of the ancient Indianapolis Motor Speedway. Waiters expertly glide past bearing trays loaded with mouth-watering slabs of sizzling meat, giant baked potatoes, and shrimp cocktails. The place reeks of maleness. A sleek, curvy blond in a spaghetti-strap dress preens at the attention she's attracting while her spindly date in wire rims wishes he was on another planet. St. Elmo is the favorite of NFL coaches and scouts when they're in Indianapolis for the combines.

Boisterous laughter rises above the din and clatter of this busy restaurant. The bitter team rivalries and battles of the past season are temporarily forgotten. A friendly bravado emanates from these old warriors of the game, these scouts and coaches, many of them former teammates or fierce opponents, as they now break bread together, drink too much, and trade lies and war stories. Everywhere in the restaurant tables are filled with tough men, strength etched in faces that reflect the great stress and pressures of life in the NFL. Legends are everywhere: coaches Don Shula and Tom Landry, Abe Gibron, and more. This one night in St. Elmo, though, we are all of one class. There are no distinctions between head coach, owner—or a measly trainer and a flunky doctor. Tonight we are all equal, men who have come to Indianapolis to use our wisdom and savvy to scout tomorrow's great players. For this one brief night we celebrate together the respect and pride of being in the hunt on a team in the NFL.

Jimmy and I pass an agent in lizard-skin cowboy boots. He's wearing an open black silk shirt with gold chains draped around his neck. He pours wine—"chateau somethin' or other," he calls it—with a flourish for two wide-eyed college players he's trying to recruit. Everyone, including the waiters, seems to ignore him. The agent doesn't belong here. He is not part of the game. He's paid no dues. He is the only one who doesn't know it.

This ritual dinner at St. Elmo occurred every year, and after 10 years, they all begin to blur together for me. The most memorable times were in the late 1980s. Chuck Knox was still the Seahawks head coach, and he inspired a very strong sense of team loyalty. We'd come into St. Elmo like a hunting pack, all swagger, a hello to friends, but with an intense sense of team. Dinner together as Seahawks was a tradition. Besides the team meal, we'd always find one additional night to eat with the Raiders medical staff. In spite of the intense rivalry between the Raiders and Hawks, our medical staffs had become fast friends, seeing each other on the sidelines twice each year during our AFC West games. Who picked up the tab at St. Elmo depended on who had kicked whose ass during the regular season.

This tradition of getting together with the Raiders' doctors extended into the regular season, all the way down to the last game in Los Angeles before the team left for Oakland's money. Jimmy and I heard that Dr. Bob "Rosie" Rosenfeld had been struck by cancer. We took a cab over to Cedar Sinai Hospital. After we visited with him for a while, Dr. Bob insisted that Jimmy and I go to the Palm Restaurant. He called the owner from his hospital bed. We cabbed it over and had a great meal with superb service. Afterwards, the owner came up, shook our hands, and showed us Rosie's picture on the wall among all the sports stars. Then he tore up the bill. Bob died less than a week later.

This past year, the Seahawks stunk, so now it's my turn to buy. Freddie Nicola and George Anderson of the Raiders are waiting for us. Fred was Rosie's younger partner, a skilled orthopedic surgeon. George Anderson was the Raider's grizzled head trainer, the only trainer they'd ever had. A member of the Trainer Hall of Fame, he developed a protective brace to help prevent knee injuries in ball players. He's also possibly one of the funniest men alive. His pockmarked face is alive with impish humor. His silver gray hair sticks out in tufts like a mad professor's. During the season, our conversations on the sidelines before each game are quite guarded. No way would either of us tip our hand about our team's injuries! But after the season, at these dinners, we laugh about all the shit we've hidden from each other.

George is in a good mood, and I think this evening's meal may be worth my picking up the tab. A tuxedoed waiter whisks by and deposits at our table an order of shrimp cocktail drenched in the famous St. Elmo horseradish cocktail sauce. Jimmy and I have fallen prey before, so we discreetly clean the excess sauce from each shrimp. But it's Freddie's first trip to St. Elmo. He dives right in and spends the remainder of the meal wiping his watery eyes and sneezing. Much water is consumed. We trade war stories as we work our way through large porterhouse steaks and a bottle of 1984 Silver Oak cabernet. George spins a yarn about the defensive back Lester Hayes and his dog. George claims that the dog stutters, just like Lester. George's ridiculous "b-b-b-bow w-w-w-wow wows" nearly leave us convulsing on the floor. We finish the meal with Partagas cigars and a nice 1977 Fonseca. George gives me a pat on the back and a handshake. "Doc, I'm the only guy in this room who can shake your hand and have a bowel movement at the same time." He giggles and winks. Then he points to the colostomy bag under his shirt, evidence of the tremendous stress faced by a trainer who dedicates his life to the NFL.

It's Thursday morning, and sleepy doctors and trainers stumble out of their hotels. We trudge through the slush and snow across the street to the Hoosier Dome (now, thanks to a few million dollars of sponsorship money, the RCA Dome). This indoor facility is perfect for scouting the 400-odd college athletes who will show up at the invitation of the NFL. It's five A.M. on the West Coast. The East Coast docs are bright-eyed and bushy-tailed, but the rest of us are nursing black coffee and still trying to orient ourselves as to person, place, and time. There is nothing like lying awake all night trying to digest a giant piece of porterhouse and combing the cigar off your tongue every hour. Jimmy gets me an extra doughnut, mother hen that he is, and rubs at his own bleary eyes. George's face looks like a rubber Halloween mask. He vows to never eat the St. Elmo horseradish sauce again, or else he'll run out of colostomy bags before the second day of combines.

By agreement, the 30 teams have been divided into seven groups. Some of these seven groups, including ours, reflect the old combines of the early 1980s. We're grouped with the former members of our mini-combine—the 49ers, Bills, and Cowboys—plus the Raiders.

Most teams will bring at least three orthopedic surgeons and one internist. If a football player has had a major injury, he'll probably be examined by all 31 orthopedists. On the other hand, if a ball player comes in totally healthy, most likely only one doctor in each of the seven groups will examine him. A weird mixture of trust and paranoia permeates this madness. Jimmy and I trust the judgment of the docs in our group because we know them from the decade we spent together in the mini-combines. Also, with the exception of the Raiders, no one in our group is in our division, so we can generally rely on each doctor to be honest. As for the other groups of doctors, that's a different story. Some of the teams don't trust anyone, let alone a member of another team's medical staff. Our front office told us that at a recent owners' meeting, some of the paranoid owners actually intimated that the medical reports produced by our group are fraudulent ruses, written in code to confuse other teams. Never mind if all five of the team doctors dictated the same "fraudulent" report! Interestingly, some of the owners don't even trust their own doctors, constantly sending team officials to the physicals to check on the doctors and see how hard they're working. If you think about the managerial implications of such a practice, it's little wonder these same owners have never been to the playoffs.

The second reason why every team doctor might choose to examine a player is that surgeons have honest differences of opinion when it comes to which injuries are important and which aren't. For instance, when Anthony Munoz came out of USC with a history of knee operations, he got a real hard look from every doctor at the combines. Five major knee operations! This represented a significant gamble for any team that considered drafting Munoz. There was a good chance his injuries had diminished his potential playing time and shortened his career. Worst-case scenario: maybe he would hurt his gimp knee in his first training camp. Maybe he would never play a down in the NFL. There were plenty of snickers among the combine doctors when the Cincinnati Bengals took Munoz in the first round of the 1980 draft. However, after Munoz spent more than a decade in professional football and made eleven appearances in the Pro Bowl, Cincinnati got the last laugh. Some of the things we can't measure at combines are heart, confidence, focus, and determination. Every draft day since 1980, Chuck Knox was kind enough to point out that I had flunked Anthony Munoz. Medicine is not an exact science.

When it's time to begin, a herd of offensive linemen shuffle tentatively into our exam room. They gawk at the examination tables like frogs looking at dissection trays. The trainers sort them out like border collies herding sheep. Before long, each lineman has been herded to one of our groups' four exam tables. My first lineman slips up onto the table with a grunt. He's wearing a white shirt with "O.L. #65" written across the back in big, black letters. This designates him as an offensive lineman. He nonchalantly flips me his medical chart and strips off his white T-shirt. He stretches out his massive chest and flexes his arms. Eight knuckles pop. Above this mound of muscle, two youthful, nervous eyes peer from beneath a buzz cut. His chart contains his collegiate medical history, recorded the night before by sports-medicine fellows and trainers. There are also X rays and the results of preliminary studies: height, weight, and Cybex scores (strength testing in the legs). As he slouches on the table, a hairy roll of fat droops over his waistband. Perspiration runs down the inside of each arm, belying his studied nonchalance.

We check out his Cybex scores, computerized printouts of strength and power testing in his legs for the quadriceps and hamstring muscles. In a normal pair of legs, each will have equal strength. If one leg tests weaker than the other, something may be wrong—a past injury, an old hamstring tear, or perhaps an undiagnosed or hidden knee injury. Most players have been coached by their agents to cover up or make light of injuries, but the Cybex doesn't lie. I set aside this player's abnormal Cybex scores and begin the exam.

"Hi, I'm the doctor from the Seahawks. I need to ask you some questions and examine you. Okay?" He nods. "You ever been knocked out?"

"No, sir."

"Not even a ding?"

"Well, I got my bell rung in the MSU game. I missed one series."

"How about a stinger. You know, a burner running down your arm?"

"None, sir."

"Your arms, any shoulder problems?"

"No, sir."

"What're you benching these days?"

"Four and a quarter." He grins, proud.

"How much does your back bother you?"

He starts. How could I know his back hurts? Actually, I don't. Sometimes I just make statements and let the player dig his own hole. "It doesn't much."

"Not even when you lift?"

He shifts nervously. "Well, it gets a little tight is all."

"You got any pains going down your legs?" I'm looking for a history of a ruptured disc.

"No, sir."

"How about your legs? You ever been operated on?"

"Just my junior year, Doc. They took out a little cartilage is all. Said I'd be fine. It was just a scope."

"Yeah, but it says here you play with a brace on your knee." I look up from the chart. The trainers have taken meticulous notes, and the college injury record has been summarized in detail for us. "What about that?"

Two pools of sweat are now collecting on the examination table. "Don't really need the brace, Doc. I just feel better with it is all." He shrugs.

"Your knee ever swell up since the surgery?"

"Only once, during two-a-days. I was one month post-op."

"But you're fine now, right?"

"Right."

"Any ankle or turf-toe problems?"

"No, sir."

The physical exam begins in much the same way as our review of his medical history—we start at the top and work down. For an offensive lineman, the key areas are the shoulders, the lumbar spine in the low back, the knees, and the ankles. The shoulders are important because of the terrific beating they take as a player is pass-blocking in the NFL. Dislocations, subluxations, chronic bursitis, and a torn rotator cuff are common injuries in the O-line. If you draft an offensive lineman who has a bad shoulder, you've probably just wasted a pick. A lot of care goes into examining their shoulders.

Next we look at the lower back. An offensive lineman has to come out of his crouch from the three-point stance with an arched back and then find someone to hit or block. This concentration of forces in the low back makes vertebral stress fractures common. The medical term for this is spondylolysis. Jimmy and I would just say, "He's got a spondy." This diagnosis should not be confused with a double stress fracture in the back that can lead to a "spondylolisthesis," or a slipping or unstable spine. Then there are the other lumbar spine injuries such as a degenerated lumbar disc, a ruptured disc pressing on a nerve root, degenerative spurs, spinal stenosis, and all the other variations in back anatomy that can cause severe back pain. These injuries can leave the lineman sitting on the bench or lying on the training room table instead of blocking opponents on the playing field. As a rule, all offensive and defensive lineman get back X rays. We know we'll find abnormalities in about one-third of the X rays. Our job is to combine all this information to determine whether the X rays, the history, and our exam add up to a bad back. At the professional level, most ball players will play with some pain—they're used to it. Some don't even think about it. Potential draft choices will try to hide injuries from us until they get that contract signed. In 1983, the Raiders' first-round pick, Don Mosebar, was in the hospital recovering from a disc procedure when he learned he'd been drafted.

He and his agent must have shared a good laugh. But I wouldn't have wanted to be the doctor (Rosie) who had to tell Al Davis that their first draft pick wouldn't be holding a press conference because he was in the hospital.

We examine the knees and ankles next. The offensive lineman's upper-body strength can keep a defensive lineman off your quarterback, but only if the offensive lineman can stay in front of the guy to continue blocking. He needs quick feet to keep his body in balance and to stay in front of the charging defense. Each of us is born with a certain mixture of fast-twitch muscle fibers and slow-twitch muscle fibers. The fast-twitch fibers give us quickness and explosive speed. The slow-twitch fibers give us endurance. Consider an offensive lineman who has 65 percent slow-twitch fibers and bench presses 425 pounds. What do you think will happen if he goes up against an enemy defensive end who can also bench 425 but instead has 65 percent *fast-twitch* fibers? In the first half, the quarterback will likely be running for his life or lying flat on his back. But if the offensive lineman has good technique and exercises some judicious holding, he may win the battle of the trenches when these men start to tire in the fourth quarter. The slow-twitch O-lineman with his greater endurance will probably pancake the exhausted defensive end. We don't need to perform a muscle biopsy to determine a player's percentage of fibers. The coaches and scouts will test agility, speed, and quickness. They will also look for what they call football instinct. Some guys are just always around the ball. They make plays. You can't coach that or test for it—you have to "smell" it. We poor docs can only test for injuries and decide whether they've been cared for properly, missed, or don't matter.

Muscle strength and composition are involved in joint stability and athleti-cism, but you need a stable joint to transmit the speed or explosive strength. Any NFL doctor worth his salt will pay special attention to a player's knees. If there is fluid or "water on the knee," that is nature's way of telling us something is wrong. A swollen knee with a 35 percent Cybex deficiency (i.e., that leg is weaker than the other by 35 percent) suggests trouble. Our first O-lineman of the day, OL #65, doesn't have fluid on the knee, but he does have a 23 percent Cybex deficiency. His scoped knee measures about a half-inch smaller than his other knee. He has muscle atrophy. I detect a grinding sensation under his kneecap when I have him flex and extend his knee against resistance. I can't find any signs of an internal ligament injury, but his medial collateral ligament has just slight laxity on stress testing. This could be because part of his medial cartilage was removed arthroscopically. There are no signs of a torn cartilage. His X rays look pretty normal. I call the other docs over and we examine the knee together. Since we're friends, the abnormal physical findings call for a group consultation so that everyone is aware of this potential problem, After we go over his exam, we agree that OL #65 probably did have an old tear of the cartilage as he had said. His arthroscopic surgery was probably well done and successful. However, OL #65 still has that slight residual collateral ligament laxity and some chondromalacia patella—wear and tear—under his kneecap. He is "at risk." We haven't the foggiest idea how good a football player he is; that's not our job. We do know, however, that he'll probably have some problems with the knee at the professional level. Whoever drafts him will need to provide more aggressive rehabilitation. Jimmy has been listening to this, and he groans, knowing he'll be the guy doing the rehab if our team drafts this guy. OL #65 might also need protective bracing for his knee, and he may experience further problems each year during July two-a-days. As the years go by, he'll probably miss some practice time while he's icing the knee in the training room and taking anti-inflammatory medication.

We agree on a medical grade of three. "A solid three, don't you think?" I say. Mike Dillingham of the 49ers agrees. Three means that the player passes, but there may be problems. We're essentially telling management, "Buyer beware." Or, "Don't say we didn't warn you."

"How'd I do, Doc? Did I pass? I mean, what'd you think?" OL #65 mops up the pools of sweat on the examination table and pulls his shirt back on. His anxious face demands an answer. I'm thinking, I've screwed up! I usually wish each player good luck with a handshake and turn away before they can ask questions. I guess it's okay to make an etiquette error at five A.M. on the first day of exams. Telling ball players whether they pass or not is not my job. In combine physicals, there is no doctor–patient relationship. We are hired to assess the physical health of potential employees. Not only that, my pass-fail judgment doesn't necessarily reflect the judgments of the 31 other team orthopedists. And we doctors are only one part of the equation. In addition to our opinions, the scouts scrutinize each player, reviewing game films to see what kind of plays these guys can make against the competition and personally interviewing the players who catch their interest.

They're looking for intangibles, instinct, the ability to make plays when it counts. To me, OL #65 may seem marginal medically. He could also be slow in the 40-yard dash and unable to do enough repetitions with 225 pounds in the bench press for his size and position. He may not weigh enough for his position—all of which could also have been said about Ray Mansfield before the Steelers drafted him. Of course, Mansfield turned into an All-Pro center for more than a decade.

I look up into OL #65's anxious face, knowing the difference between what it takes to pass the exam and what it takes to make it in the NFL. "Listen, you didn't fail. Okay? You need more therapy on your knee to help strengthen it. You may need to play in a brace; it just depends on how strong you get your knee and whether or not the brace cuts down on your ability to move freely. Also, your knee is going to bother you from time to time. It will gradually get worse—you know, wear out early. You need to know that most of the clubs that could draft you will probably have you sign a waiver acknowledging that you have a pre-existing knee injury that they are not responsible for. Also, that you could injure it further. You'll have to sign a waiver that you knowingly accept that risk. Otherwise, you don't fail, okay? Good luck."

"Thanks, Doc." A big grin crosses his face and he signs in relief. OL #65 saunters out of the room past the other nervous lineman with a newfound swagger. He didn't listen to a thing I said after he heard the words "didn't fail." I write down his grade and turn to the next young giant.

The medical grading system varies slightly from team to team, running on a scale from zero to nine. Any grade below three represents a major problem medically. A zero is an out-and-out flunk. A ball player who grades out as a zero has a serious medical problem, so serious that no surgery or medical treatment will ever correct the condition to the extent that it would be medically safe for that player to play football. Take for instance a football player who sustains a severe blow to the head during a college game and is temporarily quadriplegic on the field. He recovers completely, but as the injury is evaluated further, the doctors discover that the ball player has a congenitally tight spinal canal, or spinal stenosis. In pro ball, where everything is stronger, faster, and harder, his risk of another potentially quadriplegic episode is unacceptably high. There is no surgery that would adequately address this abnormality without leaving him open to severe neurologic risks in this violent contact game. The key word here is "game." Is this *game* worth risking paralysis or death?

Michael Irvin of the Dallas Cowboys was recently diagnosed with such a spinal condition. He decided that he didn't want to risk the chance of permanent neurological damage, so he retired. It would have been interesting to see how the Cowboys responded if he'd decided that he wanted to play. Other medical conditions that also warrant a zero include cardiac arrhythmias, destroyed arthritic knees, severe diabetes, and a missing eye, depending upon the philosophy and judgment of each club's team physician. The physician may be sensitive to the hopes and aspirations of an enthusiastic young athlete, but the doctor must also not forget his responsibility to protect that athlete's health and welfare.

Moving up the scale, grades one and two indicate that the player has had an injury that presently flunks him from participation in professional football. For example, a player with a blown-out knee would receive a grade of one. This may not stop a team from drafting him, if he has talent. They could draft him and have their team doctor perform the reconstructive surgery. If a different doctor performs the surgery before the draft, the team could have its own doctor assess the outcome. Regardless of who does the surgery, the post-operative player will then be given a grade of two. This grade indicates that the player has undergone major surgery and hasn't yet been rehabbed. His reconstructed knee will still need major therapy to return to normal function. If the player has both successful surgery and appropriate rehabilitation completed by draft day, his grade becomes a three. In other words, he's had the surgery and the rehab, but whether he can play, no one knows. Kevin Fagan, a defensive end for the 49ers, represents a best-case scenario under such circumstances. He suffered a blown knee during his senior year in college. The University of Miami's doctor did the reconstruction, but Fagan was still unrehabbed on draft day. No NFL team knew whether or not he could play football effectively. His grade was a two. The 49ers took a chance on him in the middle rounds, then let him sit out for a year and rehabilitate the knee. They gave him time to get his strength and confidence back. Kevin Fagan went on to have a great career with the 49ers.

Three is the gray zone of the grading system. As with OL #65, a three basically says, "We can't call it for sure—he doesn't pass, he doesn't fail." It's a grade that comes into play for any injury that leaves us doctors unable to predict whether the player's career will be affected. Consider bone spurs, a common condition among offensive linemen. Every time an offensive lineman crouches down into his three-point stance, he jams his ankle. After four years of high school and another four of college (assuming no red shirt), bone spurs form in the anterior ankle. More than 60 percent of offensive linemen will have an anterior ankle spur by the time they make it to the pros. Ninety percent of them won't even be aware of it. If that lineman sprains his ankle in the middle of the season, though, the spurs can cause excruciating pain and delay recovery. The same lineman who didn't even know he had the spurs might require arthroscopic surgery to remove them, just to get back on the field. On the other hand, he may play football for years and never complain about the spurs. Since none of us is psychic, such a condition calls for a solid three—buyer beware.

This same dilemma goes for necks, shoulders, backs, hips, knees, and even turf toe. There are a myriad of position-related medical conditions that compel us to warn the scouts, coaches, and management. An untreated torn anterior cruciate ligament in the knee of a running or defensive back is a one. He flunks. The cruciate ligament is of paramount importance for pivoting and cutting required by his position. However, in a quarterback the same condition warrants a three. Dan Marino doesn't flunk your physical because of cruciate ligament trouble. Maybe he just needs a brace and some good offensive lineman to protect him. Threes drive management crazy. Everyone hates uncertainty. The scouts are terrified to recommend drafting a three.

Sometimes a club doesn't want to advertise its interest in a player. On such occasions, we physicians will sometimes have to surreptitiously visit a college campus to more closely check out a three. In the spring of 1989, for example, my partner, Kevin Auld, sneaked down to Mississippi before the draft just to recheck quarterback Brett Favre's hip. He'd dislocated it in an auto accident, recovered, and then played on it during his senior year. The Seahawks had had terrible luck with quarterbacks prior to this draft, and the team was determined to get a good one. Besides, two years before, Bo Jackson had gotten a dead hip after his was dislocated in a game, so everyone was gun-shy. We sneaked in, examined Favre, and then sneaked out. Unfortunately, even though we gave Favre a clean bill of health, our club chose someone else. Favre is now a future Hall-of-Famer, but that's another story.

A grade of four or above indicates a reasonably healthy ball player. He may have had surgery, but he has played football since then and is therefore, to some extent, a proven commodity: his knee or whatever has stood up to the tests of battle. In addition to the threes and flunking grades, we discuss all fours with the scouts. Fours might include a player who's had a right knee scope, a left one, and then a shoulder reconstruction—yes he's healthy now, but maybe he's injury prone. A player may get a four if he's always getting hurt, if he's always a backup on the bench because he's recovering from injuries. Maybe his body is trying to tell us something. Maybe he can't cut it in the NFL. Freak injuries can and do occur to gifted players. If a guy has had three, four, or five operations before he even makes it into the NFL, do you really want to take a chance on him?

The fives are ball players who have had maybe one injury or a minor surgery, but they've recovered completely. A linebacker who had his dislocated shoulder repaired two years ago and has had no problems since—he's a five. A wide receiver who had ankle surgery in high school—he's a five. If he'd had that same surgery at the end of his senior year in college, he'd be an unknown, at best a three. But a player whose injury has withstood game conditions for a season or two is a five.

Six, seven, and eight are designations for players who have had a single minor operation or maybe a broken bone that healed when they were in high school. In other words, no major injuries. Nines are rare. If a player is good enough to be invited to combine physicals, he's probably seen enough contact over four years in college that he'll have injuries that have knocked him out of the nine range. Only a kicker has a shot at a nine—but even a one-legged kicker with a prosthetic leg could pass our physical, provided his good leg is his kicking leg!

It's mid-morning at the Hoosier Dome and players are still coming through the door. Every time I turn around, a new giant stands waiting to be examined. After wrestling with the legs of just 30 of these big lugs, our backs are killing us. Examining 300-pound linemen is physically demanding on the examining doctor's lower back. In the old days of the mini-combines in Dallas, Pat Evans of the Cowboys showed me a trick. He would have the player sit on the examining bench with his leg extended out over the table edge. Pat would cradle the player's leg between his crossed legs as he stood in front of him, using his own legs to lever the giant's leg back and forth, cranking on it to test for collateral ligament stability or a cruciate injury. This simple technique spares a lot of stress on the lower back. It also makes you look like a dog humping the player's leg. Several fellow docs make lewd suggestions as they watch me examine another leg. The endless line of big bodies continues. Soon we're all a bunch of humping dogs.

We've worked our way through the white-shirted offensive linemen. For the first time in years, we're no longer seeing greasy, pockmarked players. Maybe the random, collegiate steroid testing by the NCAA and the testing of all eligible seniors through the commissioner's drug-testing program has helped to eliminate this problem. For the sake of the players' health, we hope so. George and Jimmy joke that they kind of miss all the fat guys with zits and a sneer and an attitude. "Now all we got is just fat guys," George grumbles.

Lunchtime comes and goes. We take a break to wolf down stale sandwiches, soggy potato chips, and Diet Cokes. In the room where we eat our lunch, there's a fat guy with a burr haircut, brown pants, a blue sport coat, and white socks at our table. He doesn't speak to us, just keeps watching some doctors across the room at another table. I try to catch his eye to introduce myself and say hello, but he stands abruptly and leaves. George tells me the guy was Cardinal management, sneaking a check on their docs, making sure they didn't take too long for lunch. We shove ourselves away from the table and drag our own weary, jet-lagged limbs back to the exam room.

The players we're seeing now have a different attitude. We've finished the last of the O-line, and offensive linemen, by nature, tend to be neat. In their specialized little football world of trench warfare, everything must be in its place: The opposing tackle should be pancaked. The defensive ends may over-rush the quarterback so long as he's safe in the pocket. A delayed, stunting linebacker must be stopped with strategically staggered blocks. In the O-line's tidy world, the ball sails downfield into the outstretched arms of an open wideout while the quarterback stands free and unmolested.

But now a herd of disorganized defensive linemen swagger into our rooms. The DLs bring with them an air of derring-do, joking, pranks, and deep belly laughs. Don't be fooled by their braggadocio, these guys are smart, too. They have to read the offensive sets, sense by the formation and the whiteness of the linemen's knuckles in their stance whether a run or a pass is coming. They are ready to explode, to swim, stunt, spin, bull-rush, shrug, and play off the double teams. Their job is to wreak havoc and create mayhem, disrupt and punish. In short, they make their living knocking people down. They also spend countless hours year after year, practicing what to do after *they* get knocked down: to spring up like lightning, to strike between, around, or underneath the offensive lineman, to get a hand in, to knock down the quarterback or bat away his pass. These big guys waltz in, cocky, their charts all out of order. One clutches his X rays in a loose pile in his sweaty armpit. Another lineman suddenly curses and darts out of the room to retrieve his lost packet of medical records from his last exam. Yet another one smirks as he pulls the missing packet from under his shirt where he had hidden it.

Every now and then, I'd hear some truly pathetic and desperate stories from the players I examined. They'd be funny if they weren't so tragic. Many potential draft choices have only this one shot at success in life. They may come from disadvantaged backgrounds, they may have learning disabilities, but they do excel on a football field, and that's why they are here.

"It says here that you have a family history of heart trouble."

"Well yeah, that's right . . . in my family."

"Well, what exactly kind of heart trouble is that? A heart murmur?"

"No, sir."

"Some congenital condition?"

"Congen . . . con . . ."

"Never mind. What exactly was it, that heart condition?"

"Well, my brother, see, he got shot in the heart."

It's no fun having to give a low grade to a player who has so much riding on the exam, especially if he suffers from an injury that's been treated poorly. Every year we'd see examples of blatant malpractice in surgery performed on these young men. I remember examining a linebacker from a Division I university in Texas. You could see from the intensity in his eyes that he was tougher than nails. Our scouts had watched the game films and liked the way he was always around the ball, always making plays. He had a nose for the ball. The only problem was, he'd blown out his anterior cruciate ligament in one knee during his junior year. He came back from the operation, but then he blew his other cruciate ligament during his senior year. The problem was that the surgeon who'd repaired him had done each reconstruction backwards. This poor kid never had a chance. Should we tell him or not? It's a moral quandary for us, as we have no doctor–patient relationship here. Our only job is to represent the club for a "pre-employment physical." Sometimes our outrage overcame our reticence.

Medically, our concerns for defensive linemen are the same as for offensive linemen: namely, shoulders and knees. Also, the elbows of D-linemen take a terrific beating from arm tackling. It's not uncommon to see these players come out of college with fixed flexion contractures and stiff elbows. Bone chips and spurs will form in the joint from the repetitive trauma of sticking one's arm out into the path of running bodies. Severe arthritis of the elbow is common among older linemen. During a lineman's career, I might have to go into his arm and debride the chips and spurs arthroscopically several times.

In the late afternoon, Jimmy and I take a break during a lull between groups of linemen to stretch and walk around the Hoosier Dome. We wander the building and eventually head for the playing field. As we push through the revolving doors, a blast of air shoots through the gap, and our ears pop with the increased pressure inside the dome. This elevated pressure comes from the huge fans that keep the pliable dome roof inflated.

The offensive linemen that we examined earlier this morning are on the artificial turf, stretching and loosening up their limbs at one end of the field. They've all signed workout waivers acknowledging that they have voluntarily chosen to perform the drills that the scouts have prepared. In signing these waivers, they affirm that they are in good health, and, in essence, willing to assume the risk of any injury. These waivers are necessary because, naturally, someone once sued the NFL when they got hurt at a combine.

Before the day is done, everyone in the group will get weighed and photographed, have his height measured, his percent body fat estimated, and his flexibility determined. Unless a player has an injury exemption, he will be timed in the 40-yard dash, bench press 225 pounds as many times as he can, and receive the NFL's intelligence quotient test. There are also blood and urine tests for controlled substances. The players will also perform a standing broad jump, a vertical leap, and an agility test.

Kickers and quarterbacks can be exempted from the weight lifting if they desire, but most try, just for the hell of it. Not too many kickers can do even one rep. The agility drills are refined by position. There are passing drills for quarterbacks: short and long routes for accuracy, distance, timing patterns, quickness of release, and so forth. Later this week, the wideouts will run patterns: post patterns, fly patterns, go routes, comebacks, and curl routes. The scouts want to see their hands. Do they have soft hands, or do they have bricks? Can the receiver separate from a D-back? Speed is not the most valuable quality for receivers. Remember Hall-of-Famer Steve Largent? He ran a 4.6 forty. Soft hands and the ability to separate determine the blue chippers.

Jimmy and I watch the first offensive lineman come thundering down in the 40 yard dash. Three timers clock him with stopwatches. They joke among themselves whether the lineman's time was "wind-aided" or not—this in an enclosed dome. Someone curses and claims that he needs to reset his sundial. They all agree they've just seen at least 300 pounds of furious fat and beef. Each runner gets two attempts. Some are amazingly quick: 295 pounds and a 4.85 forty! The average for the fat boys is about 5.0 seconds. Fast doesn't necessarily mean better. It will be only one small component of what it takes to excel in the NFL. Heart, courage, leadership, and character are the qualities that portend greatness in a football player. The combines provide an assessment of medical grades and physical skills. We can't measure the intangibles.

The scouts know this and spend endless hours watching game films of prospective draft choices. They interview the players on campus and talk to their college coaches. They go back and study the game films again, observing how a given player performed against a variety of opponents. What caliber was the opposition? How will that player respond to the pressures of the NFL? Take a punter for example. He might average 51 yards per punt with a hang time of 5.2 seconds in the Hoosier Dome. But how well will he handle the ball on a frozen field with a 20-knot wind in his face and 10 charging bodies trying to smash into him and block the kick? And what if the whole playoff game is riding on his accurate, deep kick, which will pin the opponent back during the final minute of a game? Will he fumble the snap? Will he shank the stupid ball out of bounds and seven yards upfield? Does he have the focus to shut out the elements, the crowd noise, and the pressure of the enemy rush? The scouts know that the combines won't give them these answers.

Jimmy and I sigh as we leave the tryout field. Sprinkled through the stands are coaches, scouts, some owners, and "distinguished" members of the press. They seem bored. In fact, it is boring. It is not that these players are boring, or that watching fat men run the 40 is boring. It is that, to a certain extent, these examinations are more dehumanizing than interesting.

On our way back to the exam room, we pass a door with a sign that says "Agent Interviews." We glance into the room and see the same guy in lizard-skin cowboy boots that we saw at St. Elmo. His gold chains have been exchanged for a shiny sterling silver string tie, a blue silk suit, and an expensive cream-colored Stetson. He is in earnest conversation with a young player, talking rapidly and using his hands for emphasis. On the other side of the room sits another agent. He has a deep electric tan. He feigns boredom and nonchalance. He's wearing Cole Hahns with no socks, rumpled, pleated casual cotton pants, a solid gold bracelet. Under a tan cashmere jacket, he sports a black T-shirt with a Nike swoosh on it. Oh yes, and a diamond on the pinkie.

Most of the top agents wouldn't be caught dead in this room, trolling for clients. They've already had their underlings scout players and arrange private dinners with chauffeured black limousines. Many of the better players have already signed, even before their invitation to the combine arrived. The best and more arrogant players won't even show up for combines. Instead, they offer private workouts at their own discretion for interested clubs. Clubs sometimes take great risks and get caught up in the agent-generated hype. They may even fly their own doctors in for an exam, but it will not be as thorough as the physical exams that players receive at Indy.

Undertakers, the IRS, lawyers, and agents all have one thing in common: They are despised, hated, and feared, but they're also necessary. In 1990, the average salary in the NFL was $360,000. By the year 2000, the average salary was around $1,646,750. The salary cap for 2001 is about $63 million. The collective bargaining agreement, however, has divided NFL salaries between the superstar haves and the journeymen have-nots. Nevertheless, even the journeyman's pay is more money than a naïve college senior is capable of managing intelligently. Bob Wolf, a reputable agent, estimated that of those players in the NFL who have the chance to achieve financial independence, more than half will blow it. The fabulous signing bonuses and eye-popping salaries evaporate into customized Mercedes, custom stereo equipment, custom clothes, and bad investments pushed by unscrupulous agents, who take a healthy "finder's fee" for each new "golden opportunity." In 1998, the *Wall Street Journal* reported that the San Francisco 49ers' Larry Roberts had been referred to an investment expert at Dean Witter Reynolds, Inc. In a very short time, $1 million of his money disappeared. This expert disappeared, too, and Dean Witter wouldn't comment. It happens all too often. A bad agent will let a player squander the fruits of his God-given talent. A good agent can save a player from himself. Jimmy and I shrug as we look at each other and laugh. Neither of us will ever make enough money to even talk to the guy in the lizard skin boots.

The next day, we swim through the blur of another hundred nervously sweating bodies. The previous night, we sampled more single malt scotches and carefully aged meats. We'd sat through scientific papers at our medical meeting on sports injuries. Then, on to the scotch! Now jet lag and fatigue are playing across a dozen nodding heads. We begin to get irritable with each other. The West Coast doctors call this "curt rumminess." Our dictations become terse, less wordy, and my ringing headache shortens the need to hear myself speak. "T. G. Williams. He's a fullback. He has an old MCL. It's good. I went over it carefully"—this I spit out like a challenge—"Cybex is okay. Rehabbed. He is a five."

The fullbacks we just finished with were like blocky fireplugs of propulsive muscle, built to stop a blitzing linebacker or flatten a path for the running back. We glance up as running backs enter our examination room with a liquid, feline grace, pacing nervously like caged cats, ready to spring. There is a deceptive smooth softness to the muscular lines and tapered ankles of these running backs. Over the years, many of the great backs have come through these doors and flopped upon our examination tables: Franco Harris, Tony Dorsett, Barry Sanders, Curt Warner, Eric Dickerson, even "Sweetness," Walter Payton. We've seen our share of unheralded long shots too, players who either rise to fame or slip forever into obscurity. They carried names like Okoye, Butts, John L. Williams (the L stands for "L"), Brooks, and Natrone Means. Now, as I'm getting ready to examine one of these unknowns, I turn to Jimmy, who is sitting at the recording table. "Jimmy, who's this running back from Southern Tech?"

"He's a Division III, weighs 227, and runs a 4.33 forty. He's a long shot."

"Long shot? He looks like a stud! What kind of grade did the scouts give him?"

"Five of our guys ranked him between 4.5 and 5.5. Randy didn't like the way he blocks." Jimmy grins. "What kind of blocking do you think they do in Division III?"

I turn back to the player and grin. "Okay, Mr. Longshot, I want you to hop up onto the table, and let's have a look at you." Before I realize what is happening, he does a standing vertical leap, propelling all 227 pounds, 36 inches up onto the examination table. Now I'm eye to eye with his kneecaps! "Easy, big guy. Now sit yourself down and let me take a look at you." George and Jimmy stifle a snicker.

Combines are an interesting four-day dance, feinting and sparring with the truth. The instant their NCAA eligibility expires, most draft-caliber players sign with an agent. They come into our examination rooms with gold chains draped around their necks and diamonds on their fingers. "Neon Deion" Sanders could have used a wheelbarrow to haul around the ostentatious display hanging from his neck. Linebackers strut in, diamond studs in their pierced ears. Defensive backs swagger in, wearing designer sunglasses framed in gold. (Mind you, we're indoors, in the middle of winter.) The agents have coached them well for these exams. They realize that the discovery of any major medical problem will diminish their draft value and will cost the agent money as well. The agents don't necessarily tell the players to lie; they just coach them in avoiding the truth. Some players have been trained to answer like prisoners of war: name, school, years in football. They won't offer anything more.

"You ever been operated on?"

"Uh, no sir."

"What are those two marks on your shoulder?"

"I fell off my bike when I was a kid. You can see a scratch mark on my other shoulder, too."

"What about this operative report your trainer sent us on your arthroscopic shoulder surgery?"

The player's narrow-set, blue eyes get wide. "That, man? Shit. That was nothin'. Just a little old 'scope. They didn't find nothin', and I never missed playing time."

"The trainer says you missed two games."

His beady eyes shift and roll, and he runs his hand nervously through curly blond hair. It's a perm. "Don't know how he could say that. We had a bye, man. Gettin' ready for the big game against State. Ain't had a problem with my shoulder."

"You play with a brace."

"Do not."

"Listen, buddy. I don't care if you play with a nose flute. You don't want to tell me about your shoulder, why don't I just go ahead and flunk you now? You can go on to the next table."

Now his eyes look like they're going to pop out of his head. "Flunk me! Come on, man. My shoulder is fine. You can't flunk me."

"You keep jacking me around, I can do anything I want. We grade more than your shoulder here, buddy. We grade character, too."

"Hey, come on, man. Just look at my shoulder. It's fine."

At the combines, a doctor can't escape the nagging sense that something's not right. As surgeons, we embody the ethical heritage of a profession that for centuries has assessed injury, made diagnoses, and provided healing treatment. Our task is to inform our patients of their condition and the relative risks of the cure. In this combine environment, however, we are only employees of a team. We may examine someone who has a life-threatening condition, but our only job is to make sure that *our* team doesn't wind up with *that* guy on its roster. I think back 20 years ago to the time I saw a faded newspaper picture of Albert Schweitzer deep in the African jungle beside the hospital he selflessly built to help the natives. I think of Mother Teresa in India, who slept each night on a floor mat among the diseased and dying poor. I think of the talent that each of the doctors at these combines possesses and his power to heal and correct infirmity or deformity. Here, the art of our profession has been perverted. We are using our knowledge to trick athletes who are trying to steal money from rich owners in a misrepresentation of their athletic ability. My sons have just graduated from college. Is this what I would want them to become, or how I would want them treated? I gaze across the exam table at the naïve but somewhat shifty young player. Why are we doctors doing this? Like the undertakers, the IRS, and even the agents, in the game of professional football, our skills have become a necessary evil, too.

One of the most famous injury cases to come through the combines involved heralded running back Garrison Hearst of the University of Georgia. In 1993, he had slipped through everyone's exam except for one last doc, the San Diego Chargers' Gary Losse. Losse was a very thorough doctor who found a little play in Hearst's knee. Hearst had thighs the size of tree trunks, and if the muscles were tensed just right, you couldn't feel the looseness. I know I didn't.

Garrison was turning out early for the draft after an incredible junior year. Over the years, we NFL doctors have learned to be suspicious of juniors. Sometimes early turnouts lack maturity; other times they're hiding something. The player may suspect or even know that he has an injury that will affect his ability to play in his senior year. So he hopes that he can sneak by and get some big money early in the draft on the basis of his junior-year performance.

Nobody knows whether Hearst was trying to hide something at the combines. Whatever the case, Dr. Losse decided to order an MRI of the knee, and when it came back, it was very clear that Hearst had completely blown out his anterior cruciate knee ligament. A storm of controversy followed this discovery. Garrison's agent had other doctors examine him, and they suggested that maybe Garrison was unique, that maybe his lax knee explained his great running and cutting ability. He didn't need a normal cruciate! Maybe his cruciate ligament was underdeveloped! Most of us NFL doctors just laughed at those comments, but the Phoenix (now Arizona) Cardinals decided to take a chance on him. I believe their doctors warned them, but they made Hearst their number-one pick that year. Within a matter of weeks, after he'd signed a multimillion dollar contract, Garrison's knee blew, this time damaging knee cartilage as well. He finally had the surgery he should have had in the beginning and was lost for the rest of the year. Eventually head coach Buddy Ryan got impatient and cut him.

Because he went so early in the draft, our Seahawks never got a chance to draft Hearst, but I made sure I mentioned to management that he had flunked my exam! Later I met Hearst when I reconstructed his ankle with Mike Dillingham. Garrison strikes me as a man of great character and determination, and he denies trying to hide anything. Up until his ankle injury, he had been very productive for the Bengals and 49ers in recent years.

Marc Spindler is an even worse example of a junior-year early turnout who went bust. Spindler was a talented junior defensive end for the University of Pittsburgh, a really ferocious, relentless quarterback rusher who was projected as a potential high draft pick. The year after Garrison succeeded in getting drafted number one, Spindler turned out for the draft. But it was immediately obvious to the NFL doctors that Spindler had water on the knee and a blown anterior cruciate ligament. That year, ESPN decided it would station live cameras in the homes of several potential high draft picks. Round after draft round went by while Marc Spindler and his supportive family twisted in the wind on national television. Mercifully, ESPN finally shut the camera off. Whoever told Spindler that he could fool us and become a high draft pick gave him bad advice. Or maybe Spindler didn't listen to the advice he was given. He should have gotten his knee fixed and then come back and performed well in his senior year. Then he *would* have been a high pick.

It's our last day of examinations at the combine. Everyone is low on patience. Our eyes are bloodshot, and our temples throb. We are walking around like stiff-backed zombies, rustling through the charts, holding up X rays to the light, squinting to decipher the meanings in the shadows of muscle, ligament, and bone. I look up to see a skinny white kid sitting in front of me on the examination table. He has teeny-weeny hands, zits, thick glasses, and a burr haircut. He looks like an understudy from the *Revenge of the Nerds*. He grins self-consciously at my blank look and hands me his chart.

"Who are you?"

"Walters, sir. Russell Walters."

"What is this, some kind of joke? You a waiter from St. Elmo? Maybe an accountant?"

"From Texas, sir. I'm a kicker."

"Hallelujah! The kickers are here! The kickers are here!" Our group gives a collective sigh of relief. The kickers signal the beginning of the end. Usually only 10 or so are brought in, and they are the last to be examined.

Four days of exams in which 300 to 400 players are examined by 31 teams, coaches, scouts, trainers, and docs—talk about expensive! The budget for this extravaganza runs into the millions. Why? The answer is really quite simple: money and winning. But in spite of the money, the effort, the research, and the testing, every year teams draft players who never end up playing. After we slipped down to Mississippi to make sure that quarterback Brett Favre was healthy, we ended up taking Dan McGwire instead! Our scouts are the only ones who can say for sure whether the Seahawks' owner at that time, Ken Behring, insisted we draft McGwire.

And then there are players such as Dave Meggett, Dave Krieg, Joe Nash, and Rufus Porter who weren't even invited to the combines. These guys eventually became All-Pros! Somebody goofed! Fortunately, they got their chance because persistent scouts still listen to the old grapevine.

A lot of pretty dumb and pretty brilliant choices have been made on the basis of a single doctor sticking out his neck and putting his team as well as his own sports career on the line. Coach Ray Perkins made linebacker Keith McCants his number-one pick in 1990 for the Tampa Bay Buccaneers in spite of the fact that McCants was turning out as a junior, had undergone a major knee operation, and had an MRI that showed severe arthritis in his joint. Did Perkins actually believe McCants when he announced at a press conference that the "fourth best doctor in the world" had said his knee was okay? Sports medicine has never been promoted as an exact science. How can you measure courage or heart? Nevertheless, each team relies heavily on doctors in determining that its high picks are healthy and capable of contributing to the team and dominating on the field. That, folks, is what the winter meat market is all about.

TWO

The "Why" of Sports Medicine

Rabid sports fans might know how many yards Walter Payton accumulated, or how many field goals Lou "The Toe" Groza kicked for the Cleveland Browns in 1963, but few aficionados know much about sports medicine. It encompasses more than you might think. I remember a freckled six-year-old who played on the midget soccer team I coached. One afternoon on a rain-swept soccer field, he's running after a pack of boys. His shin guards are almost dragging backwards. He stops every once in a while to admire the shiny number on his team jersey. Suddenly the muddy ball squirts out of the pack, rolling back his way. Terror crosses his face as he turns away from the ball. His arms come up protectively as the yelling pack sweeps past him, kicking the ball downfield. The boy's red-faced father goes apoplectic, screaming at him to kick the damn ball. "Stop being a sissy!" I ask the father to cool it.

The boy continues to struggle until I discover that he's dyslexic. He's a visual, not auditory, learner. So I spend a little extra time on the sidelines, drawing plays and outlining the principles of soccer in the dirt. I tap into his visual ability to learn, and he's like a sponge soaking up water. Since he's the fastest little squirt on the team, I decide to play him at center forward. Later, in a game against the Cherry Crest Cougars, the ball bounces out ahead of the pack. He runs to it, dribbles downfield, and then stops, looking confused. Time seems to stand still. Finally he looks down at the ball and kicks it deliberately past the surprised goalie and into the net. I'll never forget his smile at that moment, the wonder and elation on his face.

Unfortunately, sports medicine isn't always so rewarding. Another day, I'm running late in a busy clinic. I'm seeing my own patients that morning after the post-game injury clinic at the Seahawks camp. We had a rash of devastating injuries in Sunday's game against the Broncos. I can still see the frustration in our coach's eyes as he yelled down the hall to the assistant GM about finding backups on the free-agency wire. The Seahawks' most serious injury was a backup nickel back's blown knee. On top of that, our outside linebacker had torn cartilage in his knee, an offensive tackle had fractured a metacarpal in his hand, and our tight end suffered a concussion. My office is backed up, and I'm an hour behind schedule when my nurse interrupts me in a patient's examining room. She says I have an emergency phone call from an agent inquiring about a Seahawks player. I excuse myself from the patient and take the call.

"Hi, I'm Dr. Scranton. How can I help you?"

The caller doesn't bother with niceties. "I represent your D-back, Lonnie. He says you told him he blew out his ACL and that he needs surgery." The voice on the phone sounds like it's coming out of a tin can. Whoever's calling is driving and using a hands-free car phone.

"That's exactly right," I say.

"Well, I want to know *exactly* what it is you have planned."

I hesitate. How do I know this individual is even who he claims to be? There is such a thing as doctor–patient confidentiality. I could be sued for discussing the player's medical condition. The agent reads my mind. "I've already faxed you an authorization from Lonnie to talk to me, okay?"

"Well, he's torn his ACL, like he said. And he has a peripheral tear of the medial meniscus. Our plan is to do a peripheral meniscus repair and then repair the ACL. I'd like to wait a week before the surgery, because if you charge right in and do it now, he'll get a stiff knee. Maybe he won't recover to play football again."

"What about an allograft?"

"What about it? Why even risk AIDS or hepatitis when we can use Lonnie's own tissue?"

"My sources tell me that's not a risk."

"Tell that to the patient in Cincinnati I just read about in *USA Today*. That guy got AIDS from a ACL graft. It can happen, you know."

The agent clears his throat nervously as he changes the subject. "Ah, what kind of meniscus repair are you planning?"

That's when it dawns on me. I remember this agent. He wears wire rims and an I-smell-shit smile. His handshake had been like a limp noodle when I met him at the Indianapolis combine. He wasn't even born when I finished medical school. Now he's trying to grill me like he's some kind of expert about his free-agent D-back's injury. This is a defensive back who wouldn't have even made the team if our starter hadn't blown out his knee earlier in the year. The agent's questions have nothing to do with genuine concern about his player. He thinks he's Jerry Maguire! This is a power message: "I am important, Seahawks. Don't screw with me." It's disheartening. Earlier that morning, I'd taken the time to bring out a model of the knee to show Lonnie what he'd hurt and how it should be fixed. But this agent couldn't care less about a doctor–patient relationship. All that matters to him is money. "Tell you what," I say. "Why don't you ask your source how I should fix it?" I hang up.

Simply put, sports medicine is the art and science of medicine applied to sport. It encompasses the rewarding experience I had with the dyslexic kid on my soccer team, the disgusting conversation with the D-back's agent, and everything in between.

By coincidence, sports medicine as a specialty came into being at exactly the same time that I began my medical training. Many fields are included under the umbrella of sports medicine. Psychological counselors help athletes learn how to win and how to accept loss. Internists and physiologists calculate fluid and electrolyte dynamics so that athletic performance can be maintained during prolonged, grueling competitions. Cardiologists study cardiac dynamics and arrhythmias. Sports injuries, such as concussions, ligament sprains, and fractures, comprise yet another specialty—this was my particular area of expertise. The dark side of sports medicine showed its face when a bunch of grotesquely muscular, pumped-up East German women swimmers walked away with Olympic gold medals in 1984 after their doctors and coaches discovered how steroids could enhance performance.

I remember how much I loved to watch the Cleveland Browns as a kid. What a graceful and punishing runner Jim Brown was. He had such molten explosive power, the ability to feint a shoulder drop and juke the other way, plus blazing speed to turn the corner. I remember when he'd take a bone-crunching hit, how slowly he'd get up. It seemed that he could barely make it back to the huddle before they broke for the next play. Jim Brown looked so hurt, so stooped in pain, you could hardly believe your eyes when he got the ball on the very next play and slanted off a tackle behind a Mike McCormack block. I remember when a part-time mathematics professor from Rice named Frank Ryan lofted the football deep over the right side of the defense. It arced down into the outstretched hands of Gary Collins, and the Browns won the NFL championship.

On another autumn Sunday of my childhood, I was spinning the channels of our black and white set, trying to find the Chicago Bears and Gale Sayers. Once, in an earlier game, I'd seen Dick Butkus put the most unbelievable hit on Jim Brown. It looked like they'd both accelerated into a wall. Gale Sayers was the running back for the Bears, and he had an exceptional cutback style that was distinctly different from the slashing power of Jim Brown. You could almost feel the electricity in the crowd's roar every time Sayers got the ball. On that Sunday afternoon, I watched Gale Sayers go down hard. Everyone thought he'd be back. Doctors could fix these things, couldn't they? Next year his explosive jitterbug and acceleration would electrify the crowd once again. But Gale Sayers never did come back. This made a big impression on me. Some things can't be undone.

After college and medical school, I decided to enter the specialty of orthopedic surgery. Orthopedics is that branch of medicine that deals with ailments of bones, muscles, and ligaments. This rather dry definition is sort of like describing Kim Basinger as "the female of the species." The specialty of orthopedics has become so vast and complex that there are now specialties within the specialty. For example, the human hand is so intricate that some orthopedists will spend an entire year studying it in addition to the four years they've already spent in orthopedic training. They then become hand surgeons. There are also joint replacement specialists, spine surgeons, pediatric orthopedists, shoulder surgeons, tumor specialists, and sports medicine specialists.

At the University of Pittsburgh, where I studied, a first-year resident often spent a year as a research resident in the orthopedic laboratory. This was my lot. After several months of research, I received a phone call from the Department of Education for the City of Pittsburgh. They were concerned about injuries in their eighth-grade inner-city football program. Would I consider covering these games? None of the university's residents or the local community physicians had the time. Most had little inclination to hang around a mud and gravel field sprayed with oil to keep down the dust, watching eighth graders butt heads and bounce off each other on an autumn afternoon.

I was already doing interesting work—growing chondrocytes in laboratory broth and recording the forces that it took to break bones—but I thought it would be even more exciting to get outside and become a part of the community. Warren Thompson was the research lab engineer, and he helped me get together a tackle box filled with tape, ACE bandages, tongue blades, and splints. I took my stethoscope along so I'd look official, and I stood on the sidelines getting oil on my shoes while I watched a hoard of scrambling kids run up and down the field. I was scared to death for a while, anxiously scanning the ground every time a play ended. Would everyone get up okay? They'd finish a play, and someone would be lying out there flopping around like a bass out of water. I'd run out only to find a scared eight grader huffing and puffing, trying to get the wind that had just been knocked out of him. I covered these games for several years, even during my residency. I just couldn't quit because it was so much fun. Successful coaches from these junior-high teams rose in the ranks to become high-school coaches. Soon, I was covering their games as well.

One Friday night, I had the satisfaction of seeing a player that I had treated the year before score a touchdown. The previous season, I'd doctored his knee injury on the field and then directed him to a university surgeon, at which point I continued to help on the case. My level of personal satisfaction in treating athletes was on the rise. At this time, the field of sports medicine was just emerging. Orthopedic doctors across the country had been coming together, sharing information, and working in the common interest to help young athletes recover from injuries. Don O'Donoghue in Oklahoma, Robert Kerlan in Los Angeles, Jack Hughston and Fred Allman in Georgia, and Jim Nicholas in New York were just a few of the orthopedic surgeons who had dedicated their careers to helping athletes. By this time, I'd become an assistant professor at the university. I began to help care for the Pitt Panthers football and basketball teams. These were exciting times. In 1976, Pitt won the national football championship with players such as Tony Dorsett, Hugh Green, Matt Cavanaugh, Mark May, and others. Shortly thereafter, a sensational young quarterback named Dan Marino was recruited.

Three years passed, and in 1979 a terrific opportunity came my way. I moved to Seattle, joining a group of surgeons who took care of the Seattle Seahawks. My senior partner, Walter Krengel, asked me to help him care for the team, and I learned a great deal from him. Then one day, out of the blue, he retired from the Seahawks and asked me to take over. One day, on a Sunday autumn afternoon, I found myself standing on the green Astroturf of the Kingdome, a talented running back named Curt Warner at my feet. He had the same electrifying running style as Gale Sayers. He also had a blown-out knee. I wondered if he would join the ranks of those whose dreams had been shattered by injury. Or could all the medical advances, the technology, and wisdom we'd gained in the years since Gale Sayers' injury give Curt Warner another chance?

A sports-medicine physician must place the interests of the team above his own. He recognizes that the team needs instant attention to injuries in order to be successful. During my first year of practice, I provided care for the Pittsburgh Ballet Theater. At the time, the company was small, and a principle dancer who had several parts in the ballet had injured his knee. He was rehearsing the Russian Cossack dance in *The Nutcracker*, a production which was intended to be an important statement to the community about the artistic ability of this new ballet company. The management had called several prominent surgeons, but they couldn't get anyone to look at the dancer for two weeks, at the earliest. Two weeks was a deathblow. The entire production depended on this dancer. They called me at home during dinner. Would I, could I see this man sometime soon? I offered to see him immediately in the emergency room, and two hours later, I performed a surgical removal of a bucket-handle tear of the medial cartilage. A trainer supervised his rehab, and two weeks later when *The Nutcracker* opened at Christmas time in Pittsburgh, he danced his many parts without a flaw.

It's a balancing act, but the best sports-medicine physicians are able to discern what's important and what is not. The demands on one's time and life can be considerable. If you don't keep a sense of humor, the job can eat you up. If you're not careful, the team personnel will abuse your dedication. "Ah, doc, sorry to be bothering you tonight at home. It's my cousin, see. He's coming in tomorrow for Christmas. He's got this headache condition.

Could you phone in some Percodans for him?" This from an assistant coach who has just been hired by the club. Some physicians can't draw the line. Several I know could never separate their own lives from the team. They've gone through divorces, they have no real friends, and they have no outside interests. I remember one doctor who joked to me that his wife had given him a tearful ultimatum, "It's me or your stupid team!" He was laughing about this at the combine physicals. I didn't think it was funny.

I've gone back to Seahawks headquarters at 11 p.m. to give an injection to an old veteran offensive lineman who changed his mind about getting a shot in his arthritic knee on Thanksgiving Day. I've gotten out of bed at 1 A.M. to care for a quadriplegic lineman who was hurt in an alcohol-related car wreck. And I've stopped a plane on the tarmac at Detroit International at 2 A.M. to save a player's leg when it would have been more convenient to fly home with the team and take a chance. But I haven't let my career come between me and my family. I asked my sons as they went away to college what they might want to become. They were unanimous. "Not a doctor, Dad. You work too hard!" Even so, as much as I dedicated my career to the team, I never subordinated my entire life to the team. Family always came first.

THREE

Draft-Day Dreams

Over the years, some Seahawks drafts have produced playoff dreams, some have produced ho-hum daydreams, and some have proven to be nightmares. When the referee shoots the final gun signaling the end of the regular season, it's also the starting gun for the next. Even as the release physicals are being administered and the players clean out their lockers, the Seahawks organization begins to gear up for the draft day four months later. The future of the franchise, as well as everyone's job, depends on getting the right information into the draft-day war room.

Management's first priority is to determine exactly what kind of talent we have, position by position. What will our needs be next year? All Seahawks players under contract are graded on their performance using the past year's game films. The head coach may already have suspicions about where break-downs occurred, but the offensive and defensive coordinators have to come up with a report, position by position, on each player. For example, a lot of quarterback sacks from the blind side where the left tackle resides could be regarded as an ominous sign. On the other hand, if the left tackle was a rookie, and if the rate of sacks decreased as the year progressed, perhaps next year that position might be counted as a strength. If most of the sacks were from double-team, blind-side blitzes and "dogs" by stunting linebackers and D-backs, perhaps the tight end or fullback might find that his job is under scrutiny, not the left tackle's. The team's coaches and scouts must assess our talent so that we can upgrade the weak spots with draft choices who will intelligently complement our needs.

This process gets fine-tuned even further as the head coach and the offensive and defensive coordinators consider the schemes they intend to employ next year. For example, let's say our team's defensive scheme was a three-man front (two defensive ends and a nose tackle) with four linebackers behind them. During the regular season, two of our starting linebackers blew out their knees and the third is a 12-year veteran who was always in the training room nursing stiff old veteran joints. With two surgical unknowns and an old vet, the coaches have some decisions to make! If there are several blue-chip nose tackles available on draft day, should the Seahawks consider changing the defensive scheme to a four-man front (two ends and two tackles) and not worry about possibly replacing three linebackers?

Shoring up the offense presents similar challenges. In 1983, Chuck Knox drafted Curt Warner. We had tremendous success, but then Curt blew out his knee. Dan Doornink and Eric Lane carried the load that year, taking us to 12 wins and 4 losses and another run at the playoffs. But the Dolphins recognized we had no real breakaway threat, and they stuffed the run and beat us. Curt came back, but our fullback blocking was mediocre at best. Chuck believed that our number-one need was to get better fullback blocking. The very next year in the second round we didn't draft the best player available, but chose a fullback instead. His name was Owen Gill. On paper, Owen had the right weight and the right forty time, and he'd excelled on offense in college. A smart move, right? Not really. The first law in any draft war room is, don't draft by need if the talent isn't there. Owen was a reach. He had small hands—referred to in the trade as "two bricks." He was incapable of consistently catching a flare pass out of the backfield. Did he weigh enough to play fullback? Yes. But his weight was more concentrated from his butt down into his thighs. He had a very small upper body. You could watch him in game films literally leap off his feet, trying to generate enough force to stop a blitzing linebacker. The 'backers just blew past Owen. His play in college had been structured around his running ability, so the scouts could only guess at his pass-catching and blocking abilities. Our organization took a gamble and lost. That year Owen never even made the team. The next year, 1986, Chuck finally got a real blue-chip fullback in the draft, John L. Williams.

Draft-day planning is further complicated by the salary cap. The salary cap is a league-wide, absolute maximum amount that each club may spend on player salaries in a given year. The league takes this cap seriously. Last year they fined the former owner of the 49ers, Eddie DeBartolo, $500,000 and penalized the 49ers several draft choices for hiding overspending. Each team's general manger and head coach must decide how much to spend on re-signing players and how much to offer free agents they want to add to the roster, all while staying under the cap. Inevitably, some players will have to go. Who is firmly under contract? Whose contracts will expire? Who will be designated as a restricted free agent (a player with whom other teams can negotiate, but the original team has the option of matching any offers). Who can they risk losing as a true unrestricted free agent? No team can afford to lose its top talent due to inattention during contract talks. Otherwise, all of those earlier talent assessments will have been wasted. Such inattention to detail cost one member of the Seahawks' management his job. Our center, Kevin Mawae, signed a contract with the New York Jets. His agent indicated that he had wished to re-sign with Seattle—all they needed was a phone call to finish negotiations. It didn't come in time.

Now factor into all of this pre-draft strategy the doctor's report. Mike McCormack was a meticulous general manager for the Seahawks, and he wanted the medical staff to prepare a summary medical report every year. He wanted me to stick my neck out and project who would definitely be healthy, who would definitely not, and who was in the gray zone. He wanted me to be a doctor to each of the players, with all of the ethical and moral responsibilities that came with the job. But he also wanted an accurate assessment from the team's perspective on player health and career longevity. Here's one of my final season-injury reports. In the interests of protecting the players' medical confidentiality, I've eliminated the specific year (no guessing allowed!) as well as players' names. This is the actual report that I submitted to Mike, and it will give you some idea of the violence and injury sustained by an NFL team in one year. (I start by reminding Mike what a good job I did the year before, because in the year of this report, I'm also negotiating my own new contract.)

Final 19—Season Injury Report

  I. All previous year's off-season and intra-season surgery was successful. No player during this year's season had residuals from the previous season's injury.
 II. Total intra-season operations—14 cases.
III. Total off-season spring minor operations—14 cases.
 IV. Total fractured bones during the season: Four fractures.
  V. Details of the season injuries and surgeries.

1. **Linebacker**
   Right arthroscopic lateral menisectomy.
   Repair fractured fibula.
2. **Linebacker**
   Fractured right scapula.
3. **Offensive guard**
   Fractured tibial joint surface, arthroscopically debrided.
4. **Linebacker**
   Torn anterior cruciate ligament, torn lateral meniscus.
5. **Defensive end**
   Torn right lateral meniscus, arthroscopically resected.
6. **Linebacker**
   Arthroscopic debridement damaged articular surface, femur.
   Myositis ossificans, left quadriceps (thigh).
7. **Punter**
   Recurrent back spasms (old spinal fusion).
8. **Offensive lineman**
   Right arthroscopic ankle debridement.
   Left arthroscopic ankle debridement.
9. **Offensive center**
   Arthroscopic partial lateral menisectomy.
10. **Tight end**
    Arthroscopic partial lateral menisectomy.
    Left arthroscopic ankle debridement.
11. **Kicker**
    Chronic back spasms, degenerative arthritis lumbar spine.
12. **Defensive back**
    Diagnostic arthroscopy status post-severe knee sprain—recovered.
13. **Offensive lineman**
    Left ankle spur arthroscopic debridement.
    Left forearm fracture plate removal.
14. **Defensive back**
    Fractured right radius.
15. **Nose tackle**
    Right arthroscopic elbow debridement.
    Left arthroscopic elbow debridement.

Right arthroscopic ankle spur debridement.
16. **Linebacker**
Closed treatment of a severe groin muscle tear.
17. **Wide receiver**
Closed treatment of a Grade II/III medial collateral tear, knee.
18. **Wide receiver**
Arthroscopic left ankle debridement.
19. **Offensive lineman**
Hemi-laminotomy and discectomy for ruptured disc.
20. **Fullback**
Right arthroscopic ankle spur debridement.
21. **Linebacker**
Diagnostic knee arthroscopy for chronic knee pain.
22. **Linebacker**
Reconstruction of torn right anterior cruciate ligament.
23. **Linebacker**
Reconstruction of torn right anterior cruciate ligament.
24. **Tight end**
Repair of fractured fifth proximal phalanx, finger.

At the end of this report, I summarized for Mike those players about whom Jimmy and I had serious reservations concerning their age and ability to fully recover from injury—factors affecting their potential longevity in the NFL. These players wouldn't necessarily flunk my physical, but their performance would likely be hampered by the accumulation of injuries and years in the NFL.

VI. "Buyer-Beware" Players

Linebacker—An 11-year veteran who is always in the training room.
Defensive back—Rookie free agent. Too many pulled or tight hamstrings.
Offensive guard—10-year veteran with arthritic shoulders.
Linebacker—Complete tear of the groin muscle, his third major muscle tear in two years.
Punter—Chronic back spasms. Always in the training room.
Defensive end—12-year veteran with arthritis in several joints.

Kicker—Degenerative arthritis in the low back. Chronic treatment. Longevity?
Offensive lineman—Arthritic shoulder, ankle.
Offensive lineman—Degenerative disc disease. Ruptured disc.
Wide receiver—Three straight years on the injured reserve.
Offensive lineman—Multiple-joint arthritis. Backup at this time.
Linebacker—Always on the injured reserve, or on an airplane for a second opinion.

No matter what these players were paid, they earned it! Keep in mind, this is just *one year's* injury report. Although the average player's career in the NFL lasts about 3.5 years, most are injured time and again. Also, these injuries occur while the players are young, and the effects can be cumulative. Most of the older NFL vets I know live lives filled with pain and arthritis from years of accumulated trauma. To see the cumulative effects of this trauma see the May 7, 2001 issue of *Sports Illustrated* with Johnny Unitas on the cover.

One of the worst end-of-season injury reports that I ever filed came in my last year with the Seahawks. Dennis Erickson was the head coach. In 1996, the Seahawks had picked up Glenn Montgomery as a free agent. He'd been a veteran nose tackle with the Houston Oilers who wasn't re-signed when the team moved to Tennessee. Glenn was a soft-spoken, likeable guy and a very unusual physical specimen—295 pounds of muscle on a 6'1" body. He was nicknamed "Short Dog" for his tenacious, ferocious play in the middle of the line. I used to kid him that he was "short for his height." It became apparent during the course of the season that Short Dog had some arthritic spurs in his left shoulder that impaired his function. He was a longtime veteran by then. At the end of the season, I asked him if he wanted us to debride the bone spurs, or did he just want to retire? Short Dog didn't hesitate. "Fix it, doc. I have another good year left in me."

My partner, Kevin Auld, and I performed the uneventful surgery in January, and after three weeks to allow for healing of the wound, we sent him back to Jimmy for rehabilitation. As was standard, Jimmy first began working to help Short Dog regain motion at the shoulder before they started working on strength. At six weeks post-operative, I got an anxious call from the Seahawks training room. "Short Dog is having really weird muscle spasms, doc." Was there anything unusual in surgery to account for spasms in his shoulder and face? This was mystifying. I'd learned over the years that a call from Jimmy meant I'd better pay attention. He had a knack for smelling trouble, and his alertness usually saved a player from getting into trouble. I told Jimmy to send Short Dog over, stat. "Let's have a look."

Short Dog came in, quiet as usual. The first thing I checked was his surgical incision. I was worried that perhaps he'd contracted an unusual wound infection or abscess that was somehow putting pressure on the nerves, causing muscle spasms. But his wound looked normal, and he had no temperature. I then examined the massive deltoid and biceps muscles of his left shoulder. Combined, they were probably bigger than my entire buttock and thigh. His muscles had a curious appearance. His massive shoulder looked like a bag of worms, all crawling and wiggling in different directions under the skin. I asked Glenn to stick out his tongue. His tongue muscles crawled and undulated in the same uncontrolled fashion. Our team physiatrist, Stan Herring, happened by. He specialized in nerves and muscular disorders. I asked him to have a look. After he examined Short Dog, we went into a small conference room. Privately, we both recoiled in horror. It was apparent that Glenn had been stricken with amyotrophic lateral sclerosis—Lou Gehrig's Disease. We referred Glenn to a consultant neurologist who confirmed our fears. The neurologist stated there was no known cure, perhaps only some experimental medicine. We told Short Dog we would do everything in our power to help, but that his fate was in the hands of God. I called Dennis to give him the news, and we urged team support and compassion. Glenn decided to go back to Houston where he'd settled with his family. Not many months later, he died.

In happier years, Mike McCormack would go over the end-of-the-season reports with me, grilling me on our team's healthy players and the buyer-bewares. After that, the medical team, trainers, and scouts would all sit down together in March to go over February's combine results. By this time, the medical charts and scouting reports of the 300+ potential draft choices had been completed. The Cybex data, 40-yard-dash times, flexibility testing, bench-press results, and so forth, were now in one file. We'd agree on a date, and that evening Jimmy would order a selection of pizza, beer, and pop, and we'd sit down to thrash out everyone who had a grade from zero to four.

We discussed each potential draft choice, correlating their injury histories to their positions. In retrospect, it still amazes me how certain players overcame what we doctors perceived to be career-threatening injuries at the collegiate level. In spite of our fears, many players went on to dominate at the professional level. We would argue and argue over these players, playing devil's advocate with each other, trying to sort out who really could play versus who would wind up nursing himself in the training room. For example, many doctors, including me, had absolute panic attacks prognosticating the multiple knee operations that Anthony Munoz had undergone at USC. True, he was so strong that he actually broke a Cybex machine, blowing its recorder off the scale, but would that strength translate into professional football success?

I fretted incessantly over a linebacker named Billie Ray Smith from Arkansas. He seemed totally beat up: broken bones, operations, pulled this, torn that. He'd also done poorly on the flexibility tests. At the time Billie Ray was drafted, flexibility was a buzzword for injury protection. As I recall, Billie Ray could bend forward far enough to maybe touch his hands to his knees. It seemed like every other linebacker in his group was touching his palms, his cheeks, or chest to the ground! Wouldn't someone like Billie Ray tear up his hamstrings with such poor flexibility? I argued with our head scout, Mike Allman, for a medical grade between a two and a three. Eventually, Mike tired of the argument. He kindly suggested that we move on. He informed me that I didn't need to worry about Billie Ray. "He will be long gone in the draft before my little heart can even pitter-patter once in anxiety!" Billie Ray was the Chargers' first-round pick, and he went on to be an All-Pro for many years.

These March discussions also gave us a chance to compare our medical evaluations directly with the scouts' rating system. Every scout on our team independently studied game films on each player available in the draft. They would then assign each player an ability grade based on his performance and the caliber of the competition. A player who dominated at his position against other players in Division IA would obviously get a high grade. But what grade do you give a dominating Division I player in a weak conference? How about in Division II or the NAIA? Trickier still, how would you grade a really dominating player from a Division III college? Postseason bowls help scouts answer these questions. The East-West Shrine Game, the Blue Gray Classic, and the Senior Bowl give the scouts a chance to see how unknowns perform against a higher caliber of talent. The blue-chippers aren't that hard to identify. The real art of scouting involves finding diamonds in the rough in the lower collegiate levels, fourth- and fifth-round picks who turn into All-Pros.

The scouts' grading system is in some respects similar to our medical grading system. For us, anyone who scored five or higher, we didn't worry about. Like ours, the scouts' scale runs from zero to nine. Anyone below a five probably doesn't have the ability to develop into a professional football player. Anyone above eight is projected to step in and start with success in the pros. Players grading above seven will probably play. Anyone above six can be expected to see some action—probably as a backup or on special teams—and eventually have a shot at developing into a starter. For the scouts, the five grade represents their "buyer-beware." A low five indicates a player whose collegiate competition or performance on the field makes it difficult to predict whether he could develop into a professional player. The lower fives and the high fours usually wash out. They represent free-agent material at best and are not to be drafted.

In our pre-draft meetings, if a player received a medical grade of three and a scout's grade of a high four or low five, Mike Allman would usually say, "Take him off the board; we don't need the gamble," thus removing half of the medical staff's niggling anxieties with a simple sweeping sentence. Keep in mind, the free agents we pursued after the draft were still in the fives, guys like Rufus Porter, Joe Nash, Paul Moyer, and Mike Tice. But these future starters were clean, medically. They *had* to be clean before the Seahawks even picked up the phone.

Next came the big meeting in which we all sat down with the head coach (Chuck Knox), the head of scouting (until 1997, Mike Allman, director of player personnel), and the general manager (during my years, either Mike McCormack or Tom Flores). This was a no-holds-barred meeting—speak now, or forever hold your peace. By this time, Chuck and his coordinators had identified the areas in which the team needed help. They also knew a lot about the talent that was out there, because they'd gone to Indy, too. There were no sacred cows in this meeting. It was absolutely vital that scouting, coaching, and management were on the same page with regard to each player's medical and ability grades. These meetings were cordial, but very tense. Chuck wouldn't tolerate bullshit. I had to know the exact reason why a player was downgraded. Chuck never failed to mention the name Anthony Munoz. He'd turn those piercing blue-gray eyes on us and ask us to justify some guy's grade. This wasn't a challenge to our integrity or an attempt to intimidate us. He just wanted to make sure we all had it right. We often did. In the months after a draft, I'd be sure to point out to Chuck any guys who flunked our physical but got drafted elsewhere and ended up on the injured reserve.

In the first week of April came the dreaded rechecks. At the combine each year, between 20 and 40 players are either immediately post-operative or still in a cast from a fractured bone. Our physical exams at that time are meaningless. A player with his leg in a cast can't run a 40-yard dash, nor can he be properly examined. After several years of frustrating calls in which they tried to monitor the progress of such players, the scouts decided that the players had to be brought back for a recheck physical. You can imagine how ecstatic we doctors were—one more ruined weekend in Indianapolis, checking the status of injured players whom our team would probably never draft.

During the rechecks, there's no camaraderie among the doctors as there is during February's combine. The whole affair is more sullen: fly in late Friday night, grind 'em out Saturday morning, fly home Saturday night. I avoided these Indianapolis rechecks like the plague. The first year, the scouts sprang the rechecks on us with just one week's notice. Jimmy went by himself, because I was with my family on an Easter-break vacation in Hawaii. I laughed at the idea that I would actually leave my family and fly back five time zones to see 20 players, then I hung up the phone. The next year, Mike Allman gave us a stern lecture on how important it was that we had *all* the information on the draft. Kevin went the following year, then Stan. Finally, I had to step up and get it done. That was the year of Garrison Hearst. All the teams demanded a recheck on Garrison now that he had a positive MRI and the cat was sort of out of the bag about his knee. His agent had already had another doctor announce to the press that Garrison's knee was fit, but at the rechecks, there was no doubt: his knee now had a 3+ Lachman's test. Either his knee muscles were relaxed, making the exam easy, or his ACL had loosened even more. In either case, my grade was still the same as it had been before. Nevertheless, the scouts had long since decided that such rechecks had to be done in person, and that particular recheck gave them peace of mind on draft day. To me, it was a waste of time and medical talent.

Each year when draft day finally rolled around, it was sort of like Christmas for the team. We were looking at a whole bunch of packages under a tree— which ones would be ours? All the organization's knowledge, wisdom, wile, and skill went into this one event. The Seahawks rarely had one of the first 10 picks, but I would still show up early in the war room. A festive, carnival-like atmosphere surrounded the team headquarters. Delicious smells wafted from a specially catered breakfast laid out for the scouts, coaches, and medical staff. Outside, a half dozen or more media trucks were parked, bristling with satellite communications equipment. Large signs were posted to direct the reporters to the media room with its phone jacks, coffee, doughnuts, and large-screen TV. Strewn around the war room were various newspapers opened to the sports pages and their "expert" prognosticators. On TV, ESPN's Mel Kiper would be busy analyzing the action during his one day of fame as the self-appointed guru of the draft.

Each club handles this circus event differently. We had a more inclusive draft than some teams in that our war room was open to the coaches, scouts, and medical staff. Everyone was expected to be immediately available for instant consultation on a player. We had two large boards filled with names. On one wall the players were listed by ability at position, and on the other wall we listed the Seahawks' draft preferences in the order we wanted them. There was frequently open discussion. We were team. When Tom Flores was our general manager, he actually threw open discussion on four different players, inviting comment from the coaches on their strengths and weak-nesses. All the while the draft clock was ticking.

Todd Sperber, our assistant trainer, told me that when he was with Oakland, Al Davis conducted the draft in a locked room with the blinds drawn. Everyone else waited outside. All was hush-hush. For some clubs, ESPN had obtained the right to have a camera live in the war room, providing up-close and personal coverage during that team's crucial moments in the draft. The cameramen, of course, are forbidden to show the team's draft board, which outlines their talent rating and team priorities.

The action got especially interesting whenever we made a decision to trade up or down. There were a lot of television close-ups of very tense faces, a phone pressed to each ear. If we were trading down, would the guy we wanted still be there when our pick came up? If we were trading up, would the guy we wanted sign with us, or hold out and miss most of training camp? Did the trade up cost too much, or did we make a smart additional pick when we traded down? The network pundits speculated frantically as the clock ticked. When the deal was finally done, after the cheers or boos subsided, there was always a nagging worry, an itch that couldn't be scratched. Did we really get a blue chipper, or not? Usually, not even that player's first year in the NFL would yield the answer.

In 17 years with the Seahawks, I witnessed 18 drafts. We were as high as the number-two pick overall, when we took quarterback Rick Mirer from Notre Dame, a major draft bust. In 1990, we gave up two number-one picks to trade up to the four spot and drafted the University of Miami's nose tackle, Cortez Kennedy, who went to the Pro Bowl many times. We've also been through two drafts where we had no number-one pick: the one in which we took Owen Gill and another in which we took Brian Blades.

Blades's draft day was a special one for me. In 1988, we had no first-round pick, having traded it to the Phoenix Cardinals for a quarterback named Kelly Stouffer. The year before, Stouffer had held out in contract talks with the Cardinals that went from bad to stalemate. He had been their first-round pick in 1987. He seemed like a good acquisition for us, given the inconsistent play of our own quarterback, Dave Krieg, but now we had no first-round pick. Talk about feeling sick—remember that Christmas tree with all the presents underneath?

As the entire first round went by, all those talented players I'd seen in Indy were taken off the war-room draft board. In the second round, with one hour to go until our pick, there were three players with very high grades still up on the board. Problem was, all three had been grading nightmares. There was Oklahoma State running back Thurman Thomas, University of Miami wide receiver Brian Blades, and another wide receiver named Perriman. Thomas had injured his anterior cruciate ligament during his junior year. He chose not to have surgery and instead he rehabbed the knee and played superbly during his senior year. His knee had withstood the tests, but we still were concerned. The wide receiver Blades had been extremely productive for the NCAA national championship team at Miami, but he had a history of painful ankle spurs which had already required surgery while he was in college. This was worrisome. Had he already begun to wear out his ankles even before he reached the pros? Perriman had undergone surgery on a fifth metatarsal fracture in his foot, and X rays showed that the fracture had not healed. In fact, the screw that was holding it in place was starting to bend. He's also been very productive in college, had soft hands and great quickness, and claimed that the foot gave him no trouble whatsoever.

So Chuck Knox pulled me out of the war room, and we sat down in Mike Allman's office for a private meeting with Mike McCormack. We had no first-round pick, and the only second-round players who had high scouting grades were solid medical threes. After losing on the Owen Gill pick several years before, Chuck didn't want to blow another second rounder.

"What do you think, Doc?"

I said that it was possible all three could play for years in the NFL without trouble. It was also possible that any or all of them might never make it through training camp. Chuck found my reply quite exasperating and turned to grill Mike on the scouting reports. Mike didn't back down or waffle. The players' grades stood. So Chuck turned those piercing eyes back on me. "Doc?"

I decided to work the problem backwards, out loud. "Suppose we assume each one of these players ends up in a worst-case scenario. How will this affect the club?" I looked around the room and saw that I had their attention. "In Thurman Thomas's case, if he blows his knee I could reconstruct it, but he'd be lost for the year, and he'd probably run tentatively for one more year until he got his confidence back. So, worst-case scenario with Thurman is two years lost. In Perriman's case, if we assume his metatarsal breaks, it's a disaster. The screw would also break, and I'd have to split the entire bone open to get the broken screw out. Then I'd have to put the bone back together with a plate and graft it with bone from his iliac crest, his pelvis. He'd be lost for one year, at best. End of career, at worst. Now in Brian Blades's case, if his ankle spurs started to bother him, we could always treat him conservatively and nurse him through the season. Worst case, I'd have to scope him during the season, and we'd lose him for three weeks." In the end, everyone agreed that choosing Blades presented the least risk.

By the time we got back to the war room, one decision had already been made for us. The Buffalo Bills had drafted Thurman Thomas. He went on to a fabulous career in the pros, retiring after the 2000 season a likely Hall-of-Famer. When our time came, we chose Brian Blades. He had a fabulous rookie season and was a unanimous All-Rookie Team selection in 1988. As it turns out, I did have to arthroscopically remove ankle spurs as the years went by, but Brian had a tremendous career. He was with the Seahawks for 11 years and ranked second in Seahawks history behind Steve Largent in career receptions with 581 catches and 7,620 receiving yards.

The role of the doctors in the Seahawks' draft-day war room varied over the course of my career. In my early years, we didn't matter too much. At that time, the combine physicals didn't exist, and the players chosen in the last six rounds or so were acknowledged gambles. In fact, before the combines it wasn't uncommon for us to flunk one or two of the Seahawks' late-round picks. In the middle years, from 1985 to 1995, the club seemed to feel that it was vital that we be present throughout the entire draft. "Where's the Doc?" Before we take this guy, is he clean?" The organization expected it. In my final three years, though, I don't believe our presence or judgment was valued.

FOUR

Prelude: Summer Camp

Once the draft is over, it's time to concentrate on free-agent signing. Each year, between 300 and 400 seniors are examined at the combine physicals. With 31 teams drafting in eight rounds, minus a few medical flunks, that leaves 60 to 100 undrafted players out there who might have that intangible something the scouts have overlooked. In signing free-agent rookies, teams are more willing to go after players by need, gambling on long shots to address perceived weaknesses or fill holes not taken care of during the draft. After the final pick, a quick team meeting is held to review the undrafted players. Then there's a mad dash to the phones.

This is not a fruitless exercise. Each year, one or two "poppers" show up in camp, the kind of underdogs that the beat writers like to profile. They're "poppers" because the coaches' eyes pop open when they see the plays these guys can make. If he's lucky, a popper might make the developmental squad, but most free agents fade as the pressures of camp and cut-downs mount.

The first of several mini-camps opens the week after the draft. It's kind of like a team honeymoon. The rookies are wide-eyed and starstruck. "Look, Ma, I'm in the NFL . . . they want me!" The veterans, many returning from off-season surgery, are well rested. For four months the locker room has stood empty. Now it echoes with boisterous laughter. Who knows what this next season will hold? My returning patients look happy. They're back; they're in shape; and they're healed. I wander through the training room shaking hands with the vets and withstanding bone-jarring backslaps and hugs.

Despite the preseason good cheer, the vets disdainfully ignore the rookies. First of all, they're a threat. Secondly, not one of them has taken a snap in the NFL. The smiles and camaraderie are for the team; for now, the rookies are only outsiders looking in. The drills are all non-contact. Seahawks don't start banging heads or risking injury without a contract. The new players are shown the basics of the offensive and defensive formations with as much coaching in the classroom as on the field. Offensive fireworks predominate because of the non-contact. There are exciting runs, and long bombs score. Everyone gloats. "Did we do well in the draft, or what?" All those Christmas presents we picked up in April start to look pretty good.

The NFL Players Contract allows for a certain number of mini-camps, depending on the team's coaching situation. A brand-new coach is allowed extra mini-camps so the players and coaches can get to know each other. More likely than not, an entirely new offense and defense will be installed. For teams with a returning coaching staff, the number of allowable mini-camps is reduced. Teams get around this reduction by hosting "volunteer" camps. The players are encouraged to come, and the coach wistfully says in television interviews, "We need to see who *really* wants to win on this team, who's really happy here." Some players get contractual bonus money for attendance at the volunteer and spring conditioning camps, especially fatties. Some players will leave the team in December at 305 pounds and come back in May at 360 with 55 pounds of blubber! Clubs recognize these tendencies and use weight clauses to penalize players for being fat and out of shape. Remember William "Refrigerator" Perry?

When I first became involved with the Seahawks, the team had no strength coach. The weight room was primitive, and most of the veteran players either stayed home in the off-season or worked out at the better–equipped University of Washington. Eventually, head coach Jack Patera hired Johnny Kai as a motivational coach. When Chuck Knox replaced Jack, Joe Vitt was brought in as the conditioning coach. With Joe, players could forget the old days of a leisurely off-season spring with some grab-ass, yuck-it-up workouts and an occasional bench press. Linebacker Sam Merriman said, "My first year, it was made very clear to us that we were to be there and in shape once we got there. Summer camp *wasn't* when conditioning started. And if you knew Chuck Knox, there was no nonsense on that.

"You had to love Joe Vitt. He had a very East Coast personality. He was always very funny, quick-witted, and ready to flip you crap. But he also accepted your flipping it back at him. Joe was great. He would have us out there running and working out like I've never worked out before in my life. I don't mean with just weights. I'm talking mostly about conditioning. Without a doubt, I was in the best shape of my life. Cardiovascularly, I've never worked out like that before or since. I'll always remember the look on [center] Kani Kuai's face one time when Joe was working us. Extreme agony. You know that you just want to walk away from that pain, but you're waiting for the first guy to drop. You refuse to let it be you. Eventually, someone drops, and that signals that we'll slow it down a little bit."

Joe Vitt's workouts signaled the beginning of a new, no-nonsense era for the Seattle Seahawks. Football teams often win games simply by physically overwhelming the opposition in the fourth quarter. It comes down to who's in the best shape. I remember Joe's early conditioning camp. At the time, I was 35. I had just finished climbing 14,411-foot Mt. Rainier and was in the best shape of my life. Joe invited me over for an early look-see. "We're just getting started, Doc. It'll get tougher in June, but I'd like to know what you think."

Each day of the camp was different—sort of like cross training—focusing on different muscle groups and circuits. The day that I showed up at the old Seahawks camp on Lake Washington (now Carrillion Point), it was gassers and abdominals. I joined in, and we started with a lot of stretching. Maybe Joe didn't want to hurt me too fast. I was hanging towards the back, trying to be unobtrusive.

Gassers are progressive wind sprints. Ten yards at half speed, then walk it back. Twenty yards, walk it back. Forty yards, walk it back. "Stretch it out, men, an easy hundred." Walk back. "Okay, let's do some sit-ups. Hit it! We'll do 50 sit-ups." I heard some little grunts at the end, but it wasn't too bad. "On the line. Three-quarter speed this time." The whistle blew. A sheen of sweat glistened on my skin, but I was still there, and my competitive juices were flowing. *Maybe the old dog could hang in there?* But soon I was dragging a bit, sucking some wind. The whistle blew again. Another three-quarter 20-yard sprint, decelerate at the end, walk back. "Stretch it out men. That's it. Okay, hit it. Time for 100 scissors. Great! On the line, pigs. On my whistle, full speed!" The whistle blew, and then it was time for crunches, and then we ran the gassers backwards.

"Very good, gentlemen, and you, too, little piggies." This was Joe's affectionate term for the linemen. "Now let's do the whole thing one more time!" After that, I had to roll over on my belly and use my arms to push myself up. Joe offered me a helping hand. "What do ya' think, Doc?"

I looked around in a daze. "Ah, great, Joe. Just great." The players were drifting off for their individual regimens of weight lifting. I shook my head clear and mumbled something about needing to get to the office. On the way back into town, I discovered that I could not lift my leg to push the brake pedal. My right leg hung limply as well, and I could barely depress the gas pedal. I clutched the steering wheel with my right hand and used my left to lift my leg so that I could hit the brakes. The next day, I rolled out of bed, steadying myself on the headboard until my feet were firmly on the ground under me. I soaked in a hot shower, ate breakfast, and swallowed two Naprosyn with one strong pain pill. On my way to work, I was still using my arms to lift my legs into the car. I decided to call Joe and decline his kind offer of another workout.

In the early days, the Seahawks also used to hold a local free-agent tryout, open to the public. The entire Pacific Northwest had gone bonkers over the Seahawks: Alaska, Montana, Idaho, and Oregon. Everyone wanted a shot at the dream, or at least the chance to say that they had just missed. It was good publicity. The tryout was held each May at the Seattle Center Coliseum. The ads in the paper read, "So You Wanna Be a Seahawk?" Several hundred guys would show up while their girlfriends and family sat screaming in the stands. In the middle of the football field during warm-ups, I once saw a guy sitting in a lotus pose, meditating while bodies zipped all around him, shagging passes and loosening up. Another wannabe was dressed in a karate outfit, running through his katas alone at one corner of the field. Neither of these guys had signed the workout waivers, and the coaches, who wanted to get things started, hollered for them to get off the field. The karate enthusiast dejectedly wandered away. Maybe the yogi reached a transcendental plane, because one minute he was in everyone's way, and the next minute, he vanished.

The tryout was a total long-shot circus. The scouts' whistles sounded, and the wannabes lined up by groups: wide-outs, DBs, backers, and so forth. Everyone ran a 40 by group. One year, three guys dropped out with pulled hamstrings, cursing. Next came an agility test. Two more wannabes sprained their ankles. The wide-outs ran a corner route around an orange cone and caught a pass. One jammed his finger, and I had to pull it back into place. The kickers practiced at one end of the field. It was like a mini-combine.

In the end, two guys were told to report for another tryout over at the Seahawks' Lake Washington headquarters. News of the callbacks rippled through the wannabes like electricity. Most callbacks were never signed. In the four years they held these camps, the Seahawks might have signed one wide receiver, a kicker, and one linebacker. The linebacker stuck—Brian Flones. He was an undersized defensive end at Washington State, but he made the final Seahawks roster as an outside linebacker on his speed and special-teams play.

Unfortunately, he dislocated his knee in his second year, shredding his ligaments. He was the last wannabe to make the team. The liability risk outweighed the benefits of the open tryouts, and they ended after Brian's year.

While the mini-camps and wannabe tryouts were under way, management was busy trying to get everyone signed to a contract and ready for camp. You can't have full-contact practices or exhibition games with people out of contract. Also, the entire process has to be orchestrated under the salary cap.

Once upon a time, there was no salary cap. The order of selection in the draft was the inverse of the team standings in the previous year, but even so, the rich got richer, and the poor got poorer. The injured reserve list and unlimited rosters provided the loopholes that allowed wealthy teams to prosper. Any team could show up at training camp with as many players under contract as it wished. The Seahawks usually brought around 120 players to Cheney each July. These players could be carried until the roster cut-downs. If the team didn't have room on the roster for a player we wanted to keep, he could be stashed on the injured reserve. The players' injuries were phony and impossible to detect. The Magnetic Resonance Imaging (MRI) machine did not yet exist. It was against league rules to stash players, and if a team was caught, it meant a fine and perhaps the loss of a draft pick. But every team did it. At Seattle, we preferred two non-detectable injuries: a pulled hamstring or a back strain. There was no objective way for a neutral physician to tell if that "injured player" was really hurt.

For the players, lying about injuries was a no-brainer. They were under contract and had "made" the team. They were living the dream in the NFL.

They could work out with the team, and there was a chance they would be activated if a starter went down with a real injury. They knew that next year, they had a legitimate shot at the active roster. To go to another team was not worth taking a gamble.

The mechanism for catching a cheating team was the "neutral physician." For example, if one team coveted a rookie defensive end who had been stashed on another team's injured reserve, the covetous team would file a protest with the league office. The player in question then had to report to the neutral physician for a physical examination. If the doctor determined that the player was healthy, the protesting team could then acquire him. The stashing team would be fined or worse.

Each year, we put between three and five players on injured reserve with fake injuries. These were players who had sufficient talent to justify their rookie salaries and simply needed time to mature. If a protest was filed, that player showed up in my office for "documentation" of the injury. I would go over the nature of his injury. I would ask him if he wanted to stay in Seattle or go to the team that had protested. This was usually met with a laugh. Was I stupid, or what? "Just checking," I'd say. I would then show them the tricks the neutral physician would use to try and fool them. If it was a back injury, we'd get back X rays. Almost every football player's back films show some abnormality, so I'd look for a little bone spur or some minor anomaly and draw an arrow to it as if it were something important. Then I'd coach the player on his pain.

"Can you touch your toes?"

He'd usually be eager to show his flexibility, bending over and putting his hands on the floor. "How's that, Doc?"

"Look, bozo, your back is hurt. Try to remember, you can only touch your hands to your knees, it hurts so much." I'd fumble with my car keys and drop them on the floor, then mutter an apology and ask the player to pick them up for me. He'd retrieve them, eager to please. "For Christ's sake. You just touched the floor again!" A new awareness would dawn in his eyes. Now I'd sit him on the examining bench and check his reflexes. I explained to him that I needed to check the pulse in his foot as I pulled it out straight. Then I would look up, impressed. "Man, you've got an incredible pulse in that foot! Want to feel it?" He'd eagerly reach down to feel it. "Miserable bozo! You just touched your toes, again! When that neutral physician lifts your leg, you rock back in pain so he can't pull that trick on you!" At this prompting, the player would dramatically flop back and start moaning and panting—another obvious giveaway. "For God's sake, just quietly rock back and grimace." Then we'd go through the exam again.

We never lost a player or got caught hiding one. I don't say this with pride. We were no different from any other team. In fact, we were a lot like agents. We coached these players to misrepresent their health so they could continue playing on our team's injured-reserve squad. We were hired to protect the players' health and to look out for the team's interests, and that's exactly what we did. The same was true for every team. Some organizations—those that could afford the salaries—kept up to 30 players stashed on injured reserve.

The poorer teams protested the loophole, and eventually, everyone became wise to the charade. Nowadays, unlimited rosters are outlawed. Only 80 players may show up to a team's summer camp under contract. After three weeks, the roster is cut to 60 players. After the final exhibition game, it's cut to 48 players. Five rookies may be re-signed if no one else picks them up, and they can then be placed on the developmental squad. Any player placed on injured reserve before the regular season cannot practice or play with that team for the entire year. If a player gets hurt during the season, he can be placed on injured reserve, but in the course of the season, only six players can be reactivated from IR to the regular roster. These rules were a welcome change for us doctors. No longer would we be caught in the middle.

These rules also promote a greater degree of parity in the NFL, though the playing field still remains uneven. The league shares among the 31 teams and its players a percentage of the combined revenue from television contracts, stadium revenue, and money generated from NFL Properties. This shared money gets divided into the salary cap. For the 2001 season, the salary cap is $67,405,000 per team.

Getting under the cap is an accounting game in which teams find many creative ways to sign players. For example, let's say we just signed our number-one draft choice to a $10 million, six-year contract. Four million goes toward a signing bonus; the remaining $6 million is spread over six years. The contract may include annual incentives such as a reporting bonus, a roster bonus, a playing-weight bonus, a Pro Bowl bonus, and so forth. In effect, many of these "bonuses" are guaranteed. If he just shows up on time and makes the roster, he may get a half million dollars up front though his game check each week may be only $25,000.

The team can immediately deduct the $4-million signing bonus and that year's salary as a business expense. For salary-cap purposes, the $4 million gets spread over the six-year contract. Now let's say our number-one draft pick sustains a career-ending injury during his first year in the NFL. From his standpoint, getting that first $4-million bonus was crucial, because his remaining salary is not guaranteed. Under league rules, if he can no longer play, the injury-protection plan will pay him one-half of his salary the following year, and after that, he's gone. The team will still have to amortize that $4-million signing bonus against the cap for six years.

These giant salaries are *not guaranteed*! Unlike professional basketball or baseball contracts, the NFL doesn't offer injury insurance or a guarantee. A signing bonus is the closest thing to a guarantee a player will see. In the past, NFL contracts were guaranteed for a large fee with Lloyd's of London. Guess who went into the red for around a half a billion dollars? With injury insurance, a veteran nearing the end of his career *benefits* from a "career-ending" injury. Let's say you're a 30-year-old linebacker with eight years in the league. You just hurt your knee. You have three years remaining on a $5-million contract, which has been underwritten by Lloyd's of London. The surgery on your knee goes well, but in the first round of the draft in April, your team selects another linebacker at your position. Think about this. You can struggle, complete a heroic rehab, and still end up getting cut, in which case you'll receive half of one year's salary—your injury-protection settlement—and then you're gone. On the other hand, if the doctor says your knee "just never came around" and you flunk his physical, that's a career-ending injury. The insurance policy kicks in, and you get that $5 million, tax-free. We're not talking rocket science, here. No wonder Lloyd's of London no longer insures NFL contracts.

The final piece of the contract puzzle involves PUP, which stands for *physically unable to perform*. If a player blows out his knee at the end of a season, in all probability he will not be ready to play early the following year. He still needs months for the reconstruction to heal and to regain his leg strength. The team must therefore declare him PUP at the start of summer camp. When the regular season begins, the team has three options: cut him, place him on injured reserve (in which case he can't be reactivated and can't practice with the team), or keep him on PUP for up to one-half of the season, at which point the team either has to activate him or cut him. If he's been practicing with the team, injured reserve is no longer an option. His salary counts against the cap, too.

So the main goal in the period between the draft and the start of camp is to get unsigned draft choices and veterans back under contract, and to do it within the structure of the salary cap. Management, the players, and the agents are all engaged in a game of financial chicken. Who will blink first?

In addition to contracts, grievances must be handled prior to the start of camp. A player who feels he was unfairly cut from the team during the previous season because he had an unhealed injury can file a grievance against the club. This mechanism was established under the collective bargaining agreement. An arbitrating service has been contracted to hear these grievances, and its decisions are final. During a hearing, management presents its side, and the general manager, trainer, and team physicians are also called to testify. The club will usually show practice or game film in an effort to prove that the player was not hurt at the time he was released. Then the player and his agent have their turn. A neutral physician will also be called to testify. One to two months later, the arbitrator hands down a decision.

The arbitrators are retired lawyers and judges, some now in their eighties, whom both the NFL and the Player's Association trust. The grievance process is a necessary one because there arise honest disagreements over a player's perception of his injury versus a club's. Each club's philosophy is different. Going on hearsay, though, some club's *are* ruthless. One team physician complained to me that his club had cut two players after the last exhibition game, one with a ruptured disc in his neck, the other with a posterior cruciate injury to the knee. He called the club to report these injuries when the players came to his office for release physicals. "Screw 'em, the general manager said. "Let 'em grieve us if they're smart enough." As it turned out, the players were smart enough, and each also sued the doctor for malpractice. I don't know how it all worked out in the end.

As the Seahawks' physician, I had few problems with the grievance system. Each year, every player who got released from the team underwent a release physical. As I did at the combine physicals, I examined them top to bottom. Each player was then asked to sign the release-physical form, indicating that I had examined him, and that he had cooperated, telling me about any and all injuries. Sometimes a player wouldn't sign. I'd ask him if he was hurt. Was there anything I'd missed? Anything that would keep him from playing football?"

"Nope."

"Why not sign to that effect?"

"Not signin' nothin'."

In my entire career with the Seahawks, I believe we had five grievances, total. Some teams had five per year. We just didn't believe in cutting people who were hurt. If a player sprained his knee in the last exhibition game before a cut-down, we still had to make the necessary roster moves. Management would ask us to predict how long it would take to get that player well. Maybe the player's knee injury was just slight sprain, a tweak. In three weeks, tops, he could be back, banging heads. In such cases, the club would offer him an injury-settlement package. He'd get three weeks salary and all expenses paid wherever he rehabbed. Therapy at the camp could be an option, but most players did not want it. When you're a player who's cut, you're out—you're a leper, disgraced, not good enough. Few players could stomach rehab in the training room of the team that cut them. Some teams used this as a ploy to get rid of a player early—they'd demand that he rehabbed in the club facility. The player's shame usually caused him to leave early.

So you might ask, if the Seahawks were so sanctimoniously noble, why did we have any grievances at all? Truth is, some players were determined to make some easy money. Once upon a time, we had a rookie linebacker. He apparently decided in the first week of camp at Cheney that he had bruised his hip. There was no objective evidence of an injury—not even a bruise. He'd spend his days singing happily in the whirlpool icing the hip, smiling bravely to his teammates and saying how, maybe tomorrow, he'd be back out there, banging heads with them. After two weeks of two-a-days, the team got one night off. The rookie was out dancing and rockin' and rollin' with the best of them. But the next day—back in the tub. His MRI was normal. His bone scan was normal. His back films were normal. Another starting linebacker came in with a grapefruit-sized hematoma over his hip. He took a shot and in two days was back out practicing.

"What do you think about a shot?" I asked the rookie.

"No way, man."

This went on for about six weeks. He was overheard telling another rookie that maybe he'd be better in time for the Chicago Bears game. That was midseason! So we cut him. Naturally, he wouldn't sign the release-physical form, and naturally he filed a grievance. The next year, the arbitrator heard the case. We had no game film to show because he'd never gone near the practice field. The arbitrator didn't know an MRI from a hole in the ground because the technique was brand new. So he heard the player, and he heard from a neutral physician. The neutral physician did not have access to our records. All he had to go on was the player's history and his complaints of pain when the doctor touched his hip. The neutral physician thought that since the player's hip hurt when he examined it, maybe three more weeks of treatment was reasonable. The arbitrator gave the player the benefit of the doubt. Luckily for the team, three weeks salary for a free-agent linebacker was not a very big bite.

Another flaw in the grievance system is that it leaves team doctors open to lawsuits. I remember many cases throughout the league where an injured player received superb care, the best that money could buy. If he'd suffered a career-ending injury, the team doctor would help him get his injury settlement or his insured salary and even testify or write reports on his behalf for a permanent partial-disability award. Then the doctor would get sued. This is a business, remember?

Most doctors, myself included, were so pleased to be part of a team that we were, to some degree, in denial about liability. We all had a vision of ourselves as caring doctors, competent in judgment and surgical technique, and we had at our disposal the best medical care that money could buy. We might expend more than $100,000 in health-care resources on a single player and never even operate on him! It was not uncommon for a player to get three, four, or five MRIs in just one season and maybe be flown all over the country for second opinions. Ask your managed care plan about that! But in the middle of his third year, after that player has been cut from the team, after the roar of the crowd is gone and there are no job prospects—

that warm, fuzzy doctor–patient relationship evaporates. Just about the time the statute of limitations is about to expire, there's a little knock on the door. "Sign here, please." You've just been served.

The press usually loved these cases. They'd just print the allegations in the lawsuit. They already knew the doctor couldn't respond, but it was a great story: The poor abused player, victim of those filthy rich, greedy owners. Of course, the press rarely reported when these cases were dropped or thrown out as being without merit.

From a league-wide perspective, the magnitude of liability was incredible. All of us physicians had the same naïve belief in ourselves that the players had about their chances of getting hurt. "It'll never happen to me." We talked about this at an NFL Physician's Society meeting. Some of the East Coast doctors' responses were almost laughable. They were full of themselves, stuffed with euphoric self-importance. They pontificated, "If you're a *really* good doctor, compassionate, and *really* caring, this isn't a problem." The next year, I got a late-night call from one of those same doctors. He was near tears, and he couldn't sleep. His name was all over the papers as the press dutifully reported the allegations—fraud, loss of consortium, reckless disregard. What could he do?

I endured lawsuits myself. Our malpractice defense team wound up reviewing tort law on a national level, specifically labor law. If you get hurt on the job, you can't sue your employer unless you can prove that your employer intended to harm you. In each lawsuit against me, the Seahawks got sued, too. And each time, the team moved for dismissal on the grounds that you cannot sue your employer or a fellow employee. That's the law in Washington State. Naturally, the Seahawks would get dismissed from the lawsuit. But guess what? As doctors, we were regarded as independent contractors—not employees, so we got to sit in the defendant's box every time a player went looking for one last paycheck.

We were facing a terrifying black abyss of liability. Say the trainer orders a new treadmill so an injured player can run on it during rehab. Say the treadmill malfunctions, and the player gets hurt. The doctor is liable, because under Washington law, the trainer doesn't exist. Anything the trainer does, he does as "an agent of the physician." The trainer can act only under the direction of a doctor. This opened a window of vicarious liability that our malpractice insurance company deemed unreasonable. My carrier decided it had spent enough money defending me against fishing expeditions by plaintiffs. They were pulling out. They "endorsed" the Seahawks, meaning they wouldn't protect any medical care I provided to the club. I'd be naked, insurance-wise.

Fortunately, our general manager, Tom Flores, stepped in. Under state labor laws, an injured employee cannot sue a fellow employee. But what if the fellow employee is a doctor? In the state of Washington, there was already a precedent. At a Kaiser plant in Spokane, there was a company doctor whose sole practice was to provide care to the company employees. He treated an injured worker who had a complication and sued the doctor. The case was thrown out. You can't sue a fellow employee, the courts said.

In light of this precedent, the Seahawks' lawyers got together with the insurance lawyers and crafted a bullet-proof employment contract making the Seahawks' doctor an employee of the team. This contract stated that the doctor's number-one priority was to provide for and protect the health of the Seahawks players and staff.

This contract has stood the test of appeal all the way to the Washington State Supreme Court. The plaintiff's lawyers whined that the doctors now had license to commit malpractice at will, but the real reason they were upset was because they had just lost a deep pocket to pick and a lot of publicity. This kind of contract has caught on and has already been upheld in several cases in California. It is spreading to other states as well, except for states such as Colorado and Indiana that have the "dual-capacity rule." This rule means that you can be an employee of a team, but if you're a doctor, a player can still sue you.

California's continuing-trauma law is another factor that can affect contract negotiations and injury settlements in the NFL. The way I see it, the law is nothing more than a way to throw a lot of money at anybody who has ever been hurt on the job. Let's say you're a retiring football player with ten years in the league. You've had concussions, sprained knees, cartilage surgery, broken bones, dislocated fingers, and so on. When you retire, you can go to court in California and claim that these cumulative injuries have led to the *end of your career*. Never mind that you might have stashed away five or ten million dollars. You now need to be compensated for the "continued trauma" of your injuries. A whole breed of doctors devote their careers to lucratively documenting every single tweak, scar, and bone spur suffered by their clients. I saw one examination report that was 15 pages long. It documented the range of motion for every single joint in that player's body. The doctor's bill for this examination was more than $3,500.00—just for a report! Does something smell funny here? The player was awarded more than $125,000. He then went on to coach for 10 more years in the collegiate and NFL ranks.

The Seahawks got stung only once by California's continuing-trauma law. We signed a veteran linebacker who'd been released by the Los Angeles Rams. He had played 13 years in the league and had never been operated upon. He was with us for exactly 10 days without being hurt when he was released. He retired and filed for the award. After reading the California doctor's report, the court awarded the player more than $100,000 for continuing trauma. Since his career had "ended" in Seattle, the judges decided in their wisdom that the Seahawks get stuck with a bill for $90,000, their share of his award. I believe this practice is an outrageous fraud. It may be legal in the state of California, but it galvanized Seahawks management to write into their contracts that players agree, on retirement, that their compensation be based on Washington State labor law, not California's.

The start of summer camp at Cheney, Washington, depended on the number of preseason games. If we were going to the Hall of Fame Game, the Japan Bowl, and so forth—five preseason games—that meant camp started early, around July 15. By contract, the veterans didn't have to report until 10 days before the first exhibition game, but the coaching staff extended "invitations" to selected veterans (usually the quarterbacks) to come out early with the rookies. Camp opened with the same hoopla and circus atmosphere as draft day. The media were everywhere. A sense of optimistic anticipation filled the camp. Our injured vets were healed, we'd signed some hot free agents, and we had a bang-up draft. Right? This would be the year.

The rookies showed up for repeat physicals, and after them the vets. These physicals were, in essence, handshakes. "Have you had any new injuries since I last examined you? Anything like a hamstring pull or an ankle sprain?"

"No."

"Welcome to the squad, and good luck." I'd shake hands with each one and look him in the eye. There was a noticeable change in the rookies' faces. No more bright smiles. The novelty of being in the NFL had worn off, and reality had set in. They were actually here, and they might get the crap kicked out of them! Some had their game faces on. Others looked like scared rabbits.

Chuck Knox opened his first training camp with a lecture to the rookies. A train track ran through Cheney, and twice a day the locomotives rolled by. "You know with my training camps, you're gonna hear that train whistle blow, and a lot of times, you're going to wish you were on that train," Chuck said.

Linebacker Sam Merriman has vivid memories of his first camp. "By the third day, it seemed a lot like hell. I think Chuck had about 80 rookies that year. Only five of us made the team. You were almost afraid to make friends with another rookie, because most likely, he wasn't going to be there for long. So my approach was, just keep my mouth shut, go to work every day, and see what happens."

I asked Sam how tough it was when the veterans showed up. "What I remember most about being a rookie was that I was very isolated. In the locker room, I remember getting dressed every day in the shower, because there was no room on the rookie side. After the morning practice and shower, I'd just go right back to the training room to get my ankles taped, because if I waited until the afternoon, any veteran could jump in front of me at will, and then I'd be late. Joe Vitt would even run us on a different field from the veterans after practice, as if we weren't good enough to run with them. We'd show up afterwards in the locker room and realize the vets were long gone. And you knew every night that your dinner was going to be interrupted by someone tapping a spoon on a glass and calling your name. And so you had to get up and sing on this little stage with Astroturf and a goalpost, and that was part of life."

Sam recalls the transition to the NFL being difficult.

"In college, you spent some time in the classroom, and you spent some time on the football field. In the pros, whether you're in the classroom or on the field, it's all about football, all day, every day. Tom Catlin was our defensive coordinator, and he was also my linebacker coach. He was known for running one of the more complicated defenses in the NFL. On every play there were adjustments to be made on the fly, depending on what happened when the ball was snapped. For every one of our pass coverages, we probably had a minimum of three or four possible adjustments, sometimes just depending on which way the running back went. I was lucky. I got to know our system really well. But we had a lot of great athletes—maybe even better than me—who mentally couldn't make the adjustments."

Sam's eyes light up when he discusses Rusty Tillman, his special-teams coach. "I loved Rusty. He was a very emotional coach. He'd played for the love of the game, and he expected that same attitude out of his players. If you blew up during a game situation, he understood that you were not challenging his authority as a coach. He really liked that intensity and emotion in his players." But Tillman was also the Turk. "During camp, he was the man, the guy who gave you the axe. If he came up to talk to you when you first walked into the facility in the morning, you knew you were in trouble. If he banged on your door at night, you knew you or your roommate or both of you were in trouble. I remember the last day of my rookie camp. I had been through all that conditioning hell, the hazing, the isolation, even playing hurt. I came in after practice and Rusty made eye contact with me and I was getting really nervous. I just kept walking, waiting, but he didn't say anything to me. The first thing I did was to run to the phone and call my dad. That moment, when I knew I'd made the team, was probably one of the greatest sports moments of my life."

Unlike Tillman, Tom Catlin used a very low-key approach. "In high school and college, I was used to being yelled at. Getting yelled at meant it was time to pay attention and get your butt in gear. But Tom wasn't a yeller. Tom talked to you with that quiet Oklahoma accent, and you had to understand that that was the same thing as being yelled at. A lot of rookies didn't get it. Even though Tom had a very gentle voice, you had better take to heart his words and understand them."

When Chuck Knox took over as the Seahawks coach, summer camp in Cheney became a much more serious affair. I'll never forget one free-agent rookie lineman who'd come into camp having missed the preseason drills with Joe Vitt. He was of little promise but great girth. (The scouts had signed him as a favor to an old coaching friend in the Deep South.) On their first day, the rookies trotted nervously out onto the field like skittish thoroughbreds. "Take a warm-up lap!" Joe said. They were so pumped up on adrenaline and nerves that they sprinted around the entire field in full gear in about 60 seconds—except for this lone, free-agent lineman, who trudged around, shuffling his feet and panting. One minute, two minutes, three minutes. He never stopped—he just kept trudging right on past us into the training room. He flopped down on the table and told Jimmy to cut off his tape and call a cab for the airport.

In addition to requiring that players be in shape *before* they reached camp, Chuck initiated "thump" drills. Jack Patera had liked a lot of contact in camp. If the running back hit the hole and didn't go down on the first hit, Patera's philosophy was that the back should twist, fight, and lunge, doing whatever it took to break free until someone knocked him down. Every practice finished with a furious, full-contact goal-line drill. As camp wound down, the whole town turned out for the hullabaloo of the final Cheney scrimmage. One year we lost three starters in that scrimmage. For Chuck, this all-out contact made no sense. "If you scrimmage yourself, you have twice as much a chance of getting someone hurt." Under Chuck, when the fully padded running back hit the hole on a trap play, the linebacker or DB was allowed to come up and give him a thump, but the instant that contact occurred, the play was dead—no second or third efforts. This approach resulted in far fewer injuries.

As doctors and trainers, we prayed that the camps and exhibition seasons would be injury-free. Our goal was to provide Chuck with a 100% healthy squad of starters for the first regular-season game. The rookies made it tough, since each one was determined to do something spectacular, anything to make an impression and make the squad. Naturally, the veterans were more inclined to stay out of the fray for most of two-a-days. They'd let those rookies pound the crap out of each other and then slip in at the end and watch them get cut.

Every summer, two or three vets would limp into the training room. "What's up?" I'd ask.

"It's my hamstring. It's tightening up. It ain't pulled, but I can feel it tightening."

"Let me see," I'd examine the thigh carefully. I'd see no defect in the muscle, no telltale spasm.

"Ouch!" The player's leg would jump.

"That hurt, huh?"

His eyes would roll, and he'd get a faraway look. "Yeah. Deep inside." I'd start to wonder if maybe I coached this guy on how to fake an injury during his rookie year.

"So what do you think?" I'd ask.

"What about letting me go through the walk-throughs, Doc? You know, I'll do all the non-contact stuff and let Jimmy treat me. I'll be ready, maybe after the second exhibition game. I don't want to pull this hammy before camp's even started!"

"And we don't want you to, either." The vet would see my smile and know he was safe. Out on the field, he could pull up and limp a little every once in a while to make it look good, muttering, "Damn hamstring." Come the third exhibition game, he'd get in for maybe one quarter, at the end, against the opposition's third string. He'd look good, showing he's still got his stuff. They wouldn't cut him.

The advent of the MRI ended this charade. If a player claimed to have a hamstring problem that we couldn't verify, and if he didn't get better real fast, it was time for a study. "Let's get a little ole MRI. You know, check and see how you're healing."

If the MRI didn't show any problems and there were no back problems either, we'd sit down with Jimmy, close the door, and have a private chat. "You see this MRI, Jimmy?" He'd nod. "No evidence of any hamstring injury, whatsoever." The player's eyes would start to get wide. "And tonight, you got to report to the general how this study came out. 'Cause the general insists on knowing how all the studies come out." Another nod. "And the good news is that the study shows there is absolutely nothing wrong."

"Nothing?" the player would say.

"Nothing." I'd show him the totally normal muscle bellies on the T1 and T2 weighted images, and then I'd give him his out. "Good thing we rested you when it got tight. Looks like you'll be able to get back into practice— that is, unless you want to tell Coach Knox you can't."

He'd give it some deep thought. "Well, how about having Jimmy *really* stretch me in the morning, put some heat on it, and give me a wrap. Maybe I'll give it a go?"

"Sounds good to me."

Injuries were our nemesis. Toward the end of camp, we'd be looking forward to opening a season that held so much hope and promise, and then someone would go down. A blown knee, a rotator cuff, a ruptured disc—any of these injuries could represent a mortal blow to the team if it involved a key player position at which we had little depth. Sam Merriman was a hero of mine. Like Job, he endured and endured and endured. A linebacker and special-teams player, he'd been drafted out of the University of Idaho in the seventh round in 1983. He'd caught the scout's eye during his senior year in the conference playoffs. In that game, the opposing team had the ball, first and goal on the four-yard line with time running out. If they scored, they'd win the game. They ran the ball four straight times, and four straight times, Sam stuffed them. The University of Idaho won the game.

Sam had terrible luck during training camp. Three times he was injured in the last exhibition game before the regular season. The first one came in Denver.

"It was my rookie year, and I got hit by 'friendly fire.' My teammate, linebacker Eugene Williams, and I both dove for a pass. We left our feet coming from opposite directions and collided in midair. Eugene missed the entire season because of that injury, playoffs and all. I knew I'd hurt my shoulder, but I played all year with a big canvas harness strapped to my chest. There was another leather strap that went around my arm to support it. I couldn't really use my arm to reach up for passes or to tackle, but I learned to ad lib and still get the job done."

In fact, Sam had played that entire season with a ruptured subscapularis muscle, ripped off his humerus. One wrong move, and his shoulder could have dislocated. We protected him the entire season without so much as a tweak. After the playoffs, I reattached the muscle surgically.

Sam's second major preseason injury was a sprained ankle. "I still don't know how I did it," he says. "One minute I was running full bore down the field, and the next instant, I was down. You guys put me into a cast, and then Jimmy would take the cast off each day for treatment. It would feel good, and then I'd sprain it again. It was the end of the season before I was 100 percent again. When you get to the professional level, physical pain becomes a very interesting thing. You learn to block it out mentally. You learn that it's just part of the game, part of the career, and if you can't deal with it, you won't be around long, or you're in the wrong line of work. The fact is, there's a lot of really big guys flying at high velocity, hitting each other."

Sam's third preseason injury ended his career. It happened in Detroit before what would have been his seventh season. I'll never forget the chaos of that day, and neither will Sam. "It was the last exhibition game of the season, and we were tied in overtime," Sam says. "I remember that they had just kicked off to us. I ran downfield to block. I had just planted my foot and my knee was locked when somebody hit Shelton Robinson and knocked him into my knee. I remember hearing the snap on my way down, and I remember thinking, 'My God, that's my knee!' In that instant, even before I hit the turf, I knew how badly the knee had been hurt. And I was thinking about my career, because I was finally going to be a starter in the NFL that year. I mean, you might expect me to be thinking, 'God, that hurts!' But that wasn't what I was thinking about at all.

"I remember sitting up a little and seeing my leg going off at a strange angle from the knee down. Right then I knew that everything had all been taken away from me. You came out, and you were moving my knee, putting it back into place. And I remember saying to you, 'Just get me off the field.' After I'd been splinted, I lay on the bench, put my hand over my eyes, and cried. I sat up for a second, and to my right I saw David Wyman, my best friend on the team, and he was crying, too. And I looked over to my left, and Brian Bosworth, my other best friend, was also crying."

Sam went into shock. We needed to get him back to Seattle, but when we got on the plane, Seahawk One, and it started to taxi, Sam experienced a sudden sensation of pressure. He took off the brace. When Jimmy and I saw how badly swollen his knee was, we had the pilot stop the plane.

"You know that I actually got a bill from Detroit Municipal Airport for disrupting air traffic?" Sam says. "I think it was about $600.00! About a week after the injury, I found a letter in my locker from Detroit. I thought it must be from some government type, some guy at the game who saw what happened and just wanted to say, 'Hey, sorry about your knee.' But it was a damn bill! When I showed it to our center, Grant Feasel, we were almost hysterical with laughter."

Nobody was laughing on the runway that night, though. Sam didn't have a pulse in his leg, and we needed to treat him as soon as possible. We went to a small hospital nearby and waited more than an hour before learning they didn't have the equipment to do an arteriogram. By now it was 2 A.M. It was too foggy to travel by helicopter, so we made a one-hour ambulance trip to the trauma center in Ann Arbor. I cut through all the red tape as soon as we arrived. "I've got a guy who dislocated his knee, and he's got no pulse. It's going on four hours. I don't mean to be rude, but I don't want any medical students taking histories, no interns or residents. I want someone here, stat, who can get my guy on an arteriogram table, and I need to know who's around from a vascular standpoint if we need them." We actually got the department chairman up at 4 A.M., and he was the one who did the study.

"I remember lying on the table, them shaving my pubic hair and sticking that needle into my artery," Sam says. "I was praying that that dye wouldn't flood out in my leg, and it didn't. It just went right on through, and down the rest of the tributaries."

Sam had ripped apart everything in his leg except for the skin, the lateral collateral ligament, and the peroneal nerve. His knee had swung open like a gate. As this happened, his kneecap dislocated, and the quadriceps ripped free. The popliteal artery had spasmed shut because of the trauma, but six hours later, by an act of God, it opened back up in time for the study. Later, we got him back to Seattle and successfully completed his surgery. He's now 11 years post-operative, and he coaches football in high school with no residuals. I recently operated on his other leg for a torn cartilage, and he actually regards the blown knee as his good one.

When the final exhibition games were over, it was time for the last players to be cut. Those final cuts were devastating for everyone, including the coaches. For almost six weeks, the players who'd made it that far had pretty much left their hearts out on the field, but someone had to go. At least half of the players who were cut would end up playing somewhere else. If they were rookies, they had a chance to come back on the developmental squad. These players were so close to making the team, they could almost taste it. *Just one more day, please, oh please, keep the Turk away.* For their entire playing careers, these men had known only success, always dominating on the field. Always, until now. "Chuck wants to see you. Bring your playbook."

We all hated it. One by one, huge, menacing men filed into my office. Some broke down in my arms and cried. I was the last stop: the final release physical. I tried to be upbeat. "You know you'll catch on. Stay in shape. They'll bring you back for sure if someone goes down."

Some players pretended to be hurt—anything to hang on a little longer. We'd carefully go over the injury.

"If you weren't here in this office, would you be practicing with the team?"

"Hell, yes, Doc!"

"There you go."

It was an especially tough time for rookie backups, who were likely to be released when we picked up proven veterans cut by other teams. Now the rookie who'd just made the team, who'd already called home to say he'd done it—now he was in my office with dark sunglasses hiding the tears. "What happened? I mean, I'd made it . . ."

"Don't worry, you'll catch on."

FIVE

Reality Check: The Regular Season

Each year, the regular season opens with incredible hype. The media frenzy starts with the August issue of *Playboy* and its NFL predictions. Then comes Dr. Z's in *Sports Illustrated.* By the end of the exhibition season, every sports tabloid, sports network, and beat writer will have some magical insight into the coming NFL campaign. For my part, I read the articles in *Playboy.*

Sunday's opening game reflects upon the organization's entire off-season: the addition of new coaches, the draft, new free agents, and the blood, sweat, and tears of six weeks of two-a-days. Will our personnel, new plays, scouting, and judgment all come together? The first team bus reaches the stadium locker room two and a half hours before game time. Then the second arrives. A third bus brings any stragglers, the owners, their guests, and the PR people who will show the guests around the stadium before the game. A palpable tension hangs in the locker room. Each year when I walked in and said "hi" to a player, he'd look up—almost in shock—and acknowledge me, but then he'd turn his focus inward again.

Tromby (our internist, Jim Trombold) and I usually camped out in a corner of the training room. It was a classic hurry-up-and-wait situation. We didn't need to be there, but we'd better be, just in case. We'd kill time reading medical journals, books, or *Gameday,* the complimentary NFL program. We avoided the coaches. I believe the tension was almost unbearable for them. Over the years, many of them came to us with severe migraines, heartburn, or stomach cramps. Their tempers flared at the slightest provocation. We gave them medication, but the only real cure was a "W" at the end of the day.

While Tromby and I waited, Jimmy and his assistant trainers furiously taped the players' ankles and a knee or wrist here and there. Jimmy was an old pro. He'd laugh with the players, joking and easing their tension. His touch was reassuring, the way he taped them with precision and confidence. In my first year with the Seahawks, the tape budget was about $50,000. When I left, it had climbed to more than $100,000 a year. Protective ankle taping was partly therapeutic, but it was also a ritual. Through the years, we offered players a variety of prophylactic ankle braces. Why get your ankle taped? Just slip on this brace; it'll save time and money. The braces provided better stability than a tape job but the players wanted to be taped, to have the trainers' healing hands on them, the application of a protective talisman.

At some point during the pre-game confusion, Chick Harris, the running-backs' coach, would yell out his first call "Kickers and special teams! Kickers and special teams!" Chuck Knox had put Chick in charge of pre-game timing. Pre-game timing was meticulously orchestrated for both teams. The kickers and special teams went first because they needed more room on the field. Next were the backs and wideouts, and then finally the whole team. The total pre-game warm-up lasted about 20 minutes—just enough running and hitting for the players to come in with a light sheen of sweat, loosen some muscles, stretch, catch a few passes, run a few plays—feel the sense of team and get ready to kick ass.

At the Kingdome, Tromby and I would go over to the "enemy" sidelines and look for their doctors during the warm-up. If it was an away opener, we'd wait for them to come to us, a matter of common courtesy. Jimmy came along to talk with their trainers. While the trainers were verifying hand signals, we'd confirm with the doctors the location of the X-ray machine, the ambulance, and which hospital we'd use if there was an emergency. This was quite important as a medico-legal technicality. If you're a physician and you attempt to render medical care in a state in which you're not licensed, you risk being held liable for practicing without a license. Legally, it's a huge gray area. Can an out-of-state doctor give a shot, pass out medication, or sew up a laceration? Nobody from the state licensing board was hanging around to check on us, but no prudent doctor would want to deal with certain injuries if there were any question of licensure. Therefore, if a visiting team's player went down, say with a severe concussion, we Seahawk physicians would assume responsibility for that player's care. The player would be transported by ambulance immediately to our hospital. An emergency

CAT scan and neurological consultation would follow. Not until the player was cleared neurologically could he fly home and rejoin his team, even if he had to stay one or two days in Seattle. Simply put, we wanted to avoid situations in which a doctor would be making medical decisions in an airplane at 37,000 feet about an injury that was evolving or unstable.

As the years went by, most of these opposing team physicians became our friends. Nevertheless, our conversations were laughably guarded. We'd talk about blown knees—from last year—or injuries we'd seen happen on someone else's team during the exhibition season. Chuck Knox had a strong admonition for everyone in the organization: "Loose lips sink ships." You never gave anyone anything.

When Tromby and I got back into the locker room, we'd usually find total confusion. At least 10 or 15 players would need their tape jobs adjusted. Some players would want to switch their shoes either for comfort or superstition. Shoe contracts made it all the more complicated. For example, if a player was under contract with Nike, but he wanted to wear a Reebok turf shoe, we'd have to spat the Reebok with white adhesive tape and have the equipment people paint on the Nike logo. The NFL also had its own shoe contract. For several million dollars a year, the league agreed to let Apex claim that its shoes were the "athletic shoe of choice of the NFL." Any player who did not have his own shoe contract would have to get an Apex logo applied to his shoe.

The equipment personnel would be scrambling to ensure that all the players conformed to the NFL uniform code: no shirt hanging out, socks pulled up, no jewelry, etc. Tempers flared easily. The string that held uniform sleeves down over the shoulder pads frequently broke, and while an equipment guy frantically struggled with the string, a player would be dragging him around as he searched for lampblack. "Where's the damn lampblack!" Four or five wideouts and DBs would want it applied to their cheeks to reduce glare. On a sunny day in an outdoor stadium, everyone wanted the lampblack.

Amidst this clamor, Tromby and I kept busy. This was the time to administer anesthetic blocks. Players came to us nursing hip pointers, bruised or cracked ribs, broken or dislocated fingers. We knew who these players were in advance, but we waited for them to come to us. We wanted them to want the shots, not to regard us as pushing them. I would have a tray prepared with all the necessary equipment: syringes, needles, Marcaine with or without Epinephrine, Betadine prep packets, and Band-Aids. Tromby and I would go into the X-ray room for privacy. The players hated the needles, and they didn't want their teammates to see them cringing in fear. Tromby usually provided each player with a clean "bite towel" so that he could muffle his screams. The privacy also served to shield other squeamish players from having to watch someone get stabbed with a needle. In the old Cleveland and Denver stadiums, the visiting clubhouses had no private room at all. Mike McCormack hated this, and he asked us to be sure to find some way, any way, to administer these injections privately.

During those 20 minutes of controlled locker-room chaos before the pre-game introductions, it felt as if we were putting the final touches on an army before war. Everywhere coaches were running after players, giving them last-minute reminders on audible calls and reads on defensive formations. There was also a mad scramble for fluids and minerals. A table was set up with special "oxygenated" water, calcium pills, potassium supplements, caffeinated pills, Tylenol, aspirin, Ibuprofen, and so on. Between the lampblack, re-taping, shots, and the scramble for meds, I'm amazed we could even field a team! I would usually take this opportunity to load at least two emergency syringes full of Marcaine in case we needed them on the field. You never knew when someone in a key position would come off with a laceration or dislocated finger. With the sterile syringes in my pocket, we could handle such injuries immediately on the field with swabbed Betadine, a stapler, or with Benzoin and steri-strips. That way, the player didn't have to run into the locker room and miss a series. At the same time, Jimmy and I would go over some of our cues, checking that the de-fib unit, the IV fluids, the backboard, and the EMT people were all where they were supposed to be. Finally, prior to the opening game only, I would rush around to see my patients, the players who I'd operated on in the past season, and I would shake their hands and wish them luck in the upcoming season. It was my own little ritual on opening day. By this time, I was ready for some Gatorade, and a couple of Ibuprofen myself.

Showtime was just around the corner. "Bring it up! Let's bring it on up." I can still hear Chuck Knox's booming voice. The entire organization would congregate amidst deafening whoops and yells. This was the moment we'd all been waiting for—the equipment people, ball boys, scouts, coaches, players, trainers, security people, and even the doctors. We'd crowd into the center of the main locker room, shoulder to shoulder, ready to begin the hunt.

It was usually Eugene Robinson whose husky voice cried out with authority, "Take a knee." The entire squad and organization knelt together, heads bowed in silence, each of us grasping a hand on each side. The circle of the team was unbroken. I could hear my heart beating in my ears. After a moment of silence, Eugene would begin. "Our father, who art in heaven . . ." Together, we would recite the Lord's Prayer.

This prayer transcended religion. It was a team moment. We prayed with the knowledge that injury or even death could await someone out there on the field. It had happened before, and it would happen again. And so we joined together in an unbroken circle of strength and unity.

In earlier years, the pre-game prayer felt empty. The Seahawks were losers, a team filled with turmoil and self-doubt. Management wasn't trusted, and poor coaching had betrayed the team. The players still had their pride and their individual goals, but there was no sense of team. So some of them hung back during the prayer. Some players stayed in the shower area, lingered in the training room or in the john. A few went through the motions of prayer.

Then Mike McCormack came in and replaced Jack Patera. Mike was a veteran. He was a man who had been in the trenches himself. He wore a Super Bowl ring, football's Holy Grail, what all players strove for. Mike was loyal, good to his word, and emotional. What you saw was what you got. When he took over for Patera as temporary head coach, he caught the attention of those alienated players. "Bring it up!" he hollered before the first game. The players milled around in confusion. Some took a knee. Mike stared around the room, noting their uncertainty, and then he cried out again, "I said, bring it up!" More players shuffled over and knelt. Mike cried out once more. "I want everyone up, and I want us all up together, real close!" We all knelt and pressed forward in the crush, grasping hands. Then Mike led us in the Lord's Prayer. He had sent a message: "Team" was back. The Seahawks went out and won that game, and Mike was awarded a game ball by acclamation of the team. Mike's message resonated until the last of the veterans left during Dennis Erickson's era but then players began hanging back in the showers again, and an undercurrent of mistrust rippled through the clubhouse.

After the prayer, the coach would announce which squad would be introduced to the Kingdome crowd: the starting offense, the defense, or the special teams. None of the coaches whom I served under offered emotional pre-game speeches. These men were pros. A speech would have sounded corny to the players after a hundred or so high school and college prep talks. A degree of coaching savvy and superstition went into deciding which squad would be introduced. If Chuck Knox wanted to emotionally jack up one of the squads, that squad would get the introduction to the home crowd. If we'd won the previous week when the offense was introduced, you knew that this week, he'd introduce the offense again. In later years, when Dave Krieg kept losing games with inconsistent passing and his maddening soap-dish fumbles, Chuck knew Krieg would get booed at home, so the defense always got introduced there. The last thing any head coach wanted was to start a home game with his own team getting booed. During those days, the Seahawks offense got introduced on the road.

The team would gather in the Kingdome tunnel, waiting to go out onto the field. The noise was deafening, in excess of 100 decibels. Usually, a Kingdome sellout crowd would already be going crazy, doing the wave. It was an adrenaline moment, one of the rushes of being in the NFL. The players would all be screaming and butting heads. I can remember seeing even Tromby excited, yelling something at me. He'd be screaming at the top of his lungs, right in my face, but in the cacophony, I couldn't hear a word. Suddenly, with an even greater roar, the team would take the field. It seemed like the introduction and the national anthem took forever. Finally, it was time for kickoff.

During a game, an NFL physician must keep in mind three rules. First and foremost, you have to keep your attention entirely focused on the field. If you started gabbing or turned to watch some new scrumptious cheerleader, some player would invariably go down with an injury. If you weren't paying attention in the crush of players, ball boys, and coaches on the sidelines, it could be minutes before you even knew one of your players was unconscious or had an airway problem. Paying attention was also a matter of self-preservation. If you were distracted when a sweep came your way, you could wind up underneath four or five professional football players with your leg broken. Al Davis was knocked unconscious on just such a play in the Kingdome. Jimmy could smell trouble, and eventually, so could Tromby and I. We would watch every play like doting mother hens, and we made sure that everyone got back to the huddle, alertly and with a brisk step. The hardest areas of the field to observe were our own sidelines. A player could get knocked out of bounds, and there would be 50 bodies screening him from our view. When we didn't see everyone coming promptly back to the huddle, we immediately moved down the sidelines to find out why.

The second rule for an NFL doctor on the sidelines is to always assume you are on television. Never, never pick your nose or scratch yourself. During a national telecast, Murphy's Law mandates that a camera will swing down the sidelines after a play and catch you in the act. For the same reason, you didn't ogle the cheerleaders. Life is too short and filled with enough pain to voluntarily make a fool of yourself on national television.

The third and final rule was to always be in a position that allowed a clear field of vision. For Jimmy and me, this usually meant standing on the sideline 20 to 30 yards behind our offense and the defense. This vantage point allowed us to see the plays develop and to see if someone got chopped, ear-holed, or shivered at the instant of contact. On offense, the teams would be moving away from us, and on defense, they'd be coming toward us. We also maintained constant field observation of our quarterback, who was the object of much violent attention.

We'd heard that some teams' narcissistic head coaches demanded that no one be within 10 yards of them as they paced up and down the field. Those coaches knew that the television cameras would be on them, and they wanted their manly frustrations, rages, and joys to be showcased without the interference of other bodies. When Dennis Erickson took over the Seahawks, he had Jimmy instruct us that the following field positioning was mandatory: one doctor would be at each 35-yard line, respectfully stationed five yards behind the trainer. The doctor would go out onto the field only if the trainer called him, and only the trainer would deliver the injury report to the offensive or defensive coordinator. Dennis didn't want to hear anything from a doctor. For about a millisecond or so, I thought about the impracticality of these mandatory field positions, and then I winked at Jimmy. "Tell Dennis you've told us." Then we went ahead and watched the field as we always had.

Standing on the sidelines was painful. Sometimes I could feel the pressure of the Kingdome's cement floor pressing up on my legs and spine within a matter of minutes. We all wore cushioned turf shoes to dampen this constant pressure. Sometimes it seemed that it took forever for a half to end. Other times it would be over in a flash. When the halftime gun sounded, we charged back to the locker room. As we went into the tunnel, the home crowd screamed encouragement. If we were playing an away game, I never looked up. I shielded my face because of the hostile way crowds liked to throw nails, beer, and batteries down on us.

Tromby had a recurrent dream that we were so far ahead at the half that the other team called over and said that they just didn't want to come back out. Would that that ever happened! The first half was usually a very tense physical battle, a probing of strengths and weaknesses. Our scores were typically low: 7–7, 3–10, and such. Back in the clubhouse, the trainers and I would push fluids and minerals. The trainers might re-tape an ankle or two. At the far end of the locker room, the coaches would huddle to go over the offensive and defensive Polaroid snapshots of the enemy's responses to our formations. Then they'd break to go over their new strategy with the players. Chalkboards were hauled out to diagram the schemes and what the coaches thought the enemy would do to counter those schemes. Chick Harris would yell into this fray, "Two minutes! Two minutes," and it was back out onto the field.

What propelled those Seahawks teams to victory? Special teams come to mind first. Hands down, Rusty Tillman was one of the better special-teams coaches ever. He challenged every player to lay it out, and he would pay bonuses from his own pocket for great hits. If his special teams stopped the enemy on a kickoff inside their own 20—bonus. Stop them inside the 10—an even bigger bonus. Force a fumble, and Rusty could go bankrupt. Blow a kickoff coverage? You risked bare-handed death. If an opposing player chop-blocked a Seahawk or blindsided him with an ear-hole, Rusty would call that player out. He'd challenge him and "MF" him all the way across the field. His apoplectic face was always screaming at the refs. Once, Rusty told Tony Burse that if he ran a kickoff back for a touchdown, he'd do a back flip. Tony did, and Rusty almost broke his neck, back-flipping onto his head and crushing a disc. There wasn't a player on special teams who wouldn't have cut his heart out for Rusty, and they believed that he would cut his out for them, as well.

In a close game, special teams would come up with an electric run back or pop the ball loose on a punt, and suddenly, it was as if someone turned on a team switch. Suddenly, the Seahawks were successfully driving, and our quarterback was actually getting protection. We'd have "mo." I've seen us score 14 points in less than 17 seconds. We'd intercept a ball and run it in for a touchdown. Then on the kickoff, special teams would knock it loose and run it back in again.

Of course, "mo" is a two-edged sword. When it really mattered, back in 1984, in the last game of the regular season, Randall "Too Hard to Handle" Morris ran back a punt for 47 yards against the Broncos. We went crazy on the sidelines—until he fumbled the ball into the Broncos' hands. It broke our back as a team, and we lost the game. Several years later, in another season-ending game against the Broncos, they intercepted us. Their side was going crazy as defensive back Mike Harden juked and cut back, trying to run it in for a touchdown. Out of the blue, Steve Largent rocketed into him and stunned him, knocking the ball loose. It was a payback for a blindside that Harden had given Steve earlier in the year. We won the game.

If special teams were the Seahawks' biggest asset, then quarterbacks tended to be our biggest question mark. Dazzling stats at the combines did not necessarily translate into NFL success, a fact especially apparent at the quarter-back position. There is a huge difference between wearing a red shirt on the practice field (when the defense can't hit you), and being a live target in a real game. During my time with the Seahawks, we went through three starting quarterbacks, all number-one draft picks, all of whom could thread the pigskin through the eye of a needle. They could pick out primary, secondary, or tertiary receivers with ease—until we went live. In a real game, when there were 11 guys on the opposite side trying to knock the crap out of them, these guys tended to choke.

For example, Jim Zorn was an incredible improviser: he could roll out, scrambling and making plays. But when Chuck Knox came in, he tried to get Jim to stay in the pocket. He wanted Jim to run a specifically designed play, to wait patiently, and to step up past the rush and fire the ball before he got hit. Jim would sit in that pocket for about one-and-a-half seconds, and the next thing you know, he was getting "happy feet." He'd start dancing around nervously, because he didn't exactly like the idea of hanging around, waiting to get killed. Jim would start to freeze up. He couldn't look off his receivers, and he started trying to force the ball. So Dave Krieg took his job. Eventually, the pressure got to him, too, and we had a revolving door at quarterback.

During the years I spent with the Seahawks, a number of different players provided leadership for the team. Take Reggie MacKenzie. He had wisdom and presence, and he was a team spokesperson. He'd been the lead blocker for O.J. at Buffalo when O.J. got his 2001-yard season. Sure, Reggie talked the talk, but he could also walk the walk. In his first year with us, he tore his rotator cuff after about one month. I made the diagnosis, but he wouldn't let me touch him. "After the season, Doc."

Curt Warner was our leader for a while. I can remember him during his rookie season, at Jet Stadium in New York City. In the fourth quarter, the game was close, and we were driving with the ball. Curt turned toward our sideline. Amidst a deafening roar, he pointed to Chuck Knox and then back at himself. He was saying, "I want the ball." We knew he was going to get the ball, and so did the Jets, but they couldn't stop him. C.W. motored through the fourth quarter and led the Seahawks to victory.

For one year, Will Grant was our leader. Our center, Blair Bush, had been lost for the season when the New York Giants' Harry Carson clipped him and blew out his knee on an interception runback. Chuck Knox brought Will in off the waiver wire. Will was a beat-up castoff, an old vet. He struck me as a con man, ferocious, probably dirty, but nevertheless a pit bull in the line. When Will was in the game, the ball moved forward. He'd take his stance over the ball, and as he bent down to snap it, he'd hocker and spit straight into the nose tackle's face. Naturally, the outraged tackle immediately decked him. Flags flew, resulting in a personal-foul penalty on the nose tackle good for 15 yards. So now Will had the nose tackle seething, itching for a chance to get even. On the next play, he would block the guy, coming in close and grabbing him by the face mask. This struggle would continue until the nose tackle grabbed Will's mask, twisting and yelling. Will would then let go, and as the infuriated tackle flung him by the face mask to the ground, the flag would come out again. "Personal foul, 15 yards, the player is ejected!" Will cut, clipped, tripped, grabbed, and bulldogged his opponents to the ground, but they didn't touch our quarterback. He was stoic, playing in pain on the equivalent of a pair of sixty-year-old knees. He loved every minute of it.

Eugene Robinson was another leader. He had presence. He was very emotional, intense, and he had the ability to come up with the big play. He didn't send out a survey or ask anyone, "May I lead?" He just led. If he was a hair late when the coach called us together for the team prayer, we'd all wait for Geno to say, "Take a knee."

Other players led quietly—no flash, no snappy press conferences, just a workmanlike dedication to their jobs. Joe Nash, "Pearl" Bailey, "Papa Fig" Newton, and "House" Ballard are a few who come to mind. Other players could have been leaders for us, but circumstances, injury, or trades never allowed them the opportunity. I offer the caveat that these are my personal observations from the sidelines. The players might have different perceptions of who our team leaders were.

You might wonder, with all this discussion of leadership, why I haven't mentioned our Hall of Fame wide receiver, Steve Largent. To my thinking, Steve was so internally focused that he was not as demonstrable a leader as many of the players I've mentioned. What he could do with his body—separating from a defender and catching the ball—was pure magic (hence his nickname, Yoda). But Steve was not as vocal as some players, which I believe is an important criterion for team leadership. Also, as a wide receiver, it's not always possible to lead. Steve could yell and cajole, but if the quarterback was sacked, that unbelievable route Steve just ran was all for nothing.

Over the years, I came to associate certain players with their jersey numbers. The old Oakland Raiders coach, John Madden, described this phenomenon once during a lull while he was announcing a football game. He pointed out that the best players became personified by their jersey numbers. It's almost impossible to think of the number 32 without imagining Jim Brown slashing through the line—impossible unless you're a Buffalo or Pittsburgh fan. Those 32s, O.J. Simpson and Franco Harris, are also in the Hall of Fame. Number 34, the all-time leader in rushing? "Sweetness." How about 14? Y.A. Tittle, in pain, on his knees, stunned and bloodied against Pittsburgh in 1964. Number 16? Joe Montana, one of the greatest quarterbacks to play the game—unless you think of Johnny Unitas, or number 15, Bart Starr. Does 80 ring a bell? Who else but Jerry Rice? How about 51? You can't not think of Dick Butkus. Jack Lambert, 58. Fifty-six could only be L.T. And so on.

Of course, much of this association between player and jersey number is strictly personal, a function of each fan's exposure to the game. For the Seahawks, certain numbers will always seem larger than life to me. Number 79? Who else chased terrified quarterbacks but Jacob Green? Number 10? Jim Zorn. And how can you think about Zorn without thinking about number 80? Yes, Jerry Rice comes to mind, but the first wide receiver I will always think of is already in the Hall of Fame—Steve Largent. I can still see his wiry, lithe body, his eyes locked on the football, the defender turned the wrong way. Largent's last touchdown catch in Cincinnati personified his career: he was totally extended, fingertips on the ball, with the toes of both shoes just inside the end-zone line.

What a personae for 45! What a great number! It seemed for years that 45 was the leading point in every bone-crushing hit, every defended pass, every interception. Kenny Easley's number just kept popping up. He was ferocious. He played with great intensity and pride. Enemy offenses built their game plans around avoiding him. Illness ended a career that should have been every bit as stellar as number 42, Ronnie Lott.

For me, number 28 could only be Curt Warner, C.W., "Killer." They called him Killer for his fourth-quarter play. By that time, he was all adrenaline and instinct. If the enemy defense was tiring, no one could find a seam better than Curt. The play would string out, he'd dart through a hole, juke the linebacker, counter the DB, and it was off to the races. Killer would put them out of their misery.

When the gun sounded at the end of that first game of the season, it was either high fives, backslapping, and hugs, or it was time for a somber gut check. Win or lose, we held a second team prayer, a sort of thanksgiving that those who were kneeling there together were healthy. The tone of the post-game prayer generally reflected the outcome of the game. If we won, the prayer was said with fierce pride, recited loudly and briskly, our hands clenching one another's at the closing: " . . . the kingdom, and the *power,* and the glory . . ." If we lost, the prayer was subdued, almost whispered.

If we won, game balls were awarded. Cheers and general camaraderie prevailed in the locker room. "Boogie" (Jeff Bryant, 77) led the cheer. "Hip, hip, hooray!" Chuck Knox would offer an admonition and words of caution: Be gracious, no gloating or boasting, say how lucky we were, how we have to go back and work harder on the things that didn't go right. Don't give the press anything to inflame our next opponent. Be humble. The only person who ever violated Chuck's rule was Brian Bosworth.

If we lost, the team went through a somber reflection. We couldn't give up eight months of momentum just because we lost one game. The coach's words were brief after a loss, brief but encouraging. "No need to panic. We still have a few tricks up our sleeve. It's just one game. We'll go back and study the film and see what we did right, what we did wrong, and where we need to coach better." Chuck never pointed the finger of blame at any player. He always said to the press after a loss, "We just need to coach a little better." If we lost on the road, his post-game clubhouse speech always closed with disdain for the "foreign" city where we'd played. "Shower-up, and let's get the fuck out of this town!" If we lost on the road, we'd stay in a different hotel the following year. If we won, we stayed at the same hotel. When we were in Los Angeles, we always stayed at the Century Plaza Hotel, because that's where Chuck stayed the night he was offered his first head coaching job with the Los Angeles Rams.

Losing an opener could be a portent of the season. In 1983, we opened against the Kansas City Chiefs on the road. Anyone who has been to Arrowhead Stadium knows how hard it is to win there. I believe their home-field advantage is worth eight points. We lost our opener, but Chuck held the team together that year to win a wild-card playoff spot. No one folded his tent.

On the other hand, in 1997 we opened *at home* against Bill Parcells and the New York Jets. We'd just gotten two number-one draft picks out of the top ten and picked up two Pro Bowl free-agent defenders. We got creamed 42–7 by a team that had gone 1–15 the year before. Our ball boys on the

Jets' sideline mentioned after the game that Parcells's coaches were laughing. They couldn't believe the Seahawks had made no adjustments at halftime. The Jets knew everything we were doing. When you get creamed in a home opener by a 1–15 team, you know the season is over before it's started. The rest of that year, the team just went through the motions.

I had a love-hate attitude toward the travel required for road games. For starters, it was the old hurry-up-and-wait. If we played any team that was at least two time zones away, we left on Friday. For me this meant a day out of the office, away from my private patients. On Monday, I would have to do two days of work while fighting jet lag. There's nothing like filling out an angry patient's insurance papers that were supposed to be done on Friday. The specter of Monday would haunt me all weekend.

The second problem was having to spend time away from my family. Professional success with dysfunctional children or a divorce is not success at all. I was very fortunate with the Seahawks under the Nordstrom ownership and Mike McCormack. They were both family-oriented. If we had an away game with an early Friday departure, I could notify Mike if I had surgical cases, and the Seahawks would arrange for me to take a flight out of Seattle on Saturday and join the team that evening. I could take care of my patients, be a dad to my boys, and share some time with my wife.

When the Behrings took over, their financial people scrutinized every aspect of the Seahawks' operations. A doctor flying out on Saturday did not compute to these bean counters. They informed me that if I wasn't on the team flight, I could fly out on Saturday, no problem. "Just buy your own ticket." In fact, I did. But this represented a new cheap attitude that soon extended into every aspect of the operation.

On the plus side, a lot of the travel was fun. When Tom Flores was coach and general manager, I enjoyed our dinners together. The team was treated like royalty wherever we went. Once we traveled to Japan: Shinto temples, Kobe beef, and karaoke! In most cities, we'd get a police escort to and from the airport. We'd drive the team buses right out onto the tarmac and board the planes off the side ramps—no lines, no waiting, and no questions. People at the airports gawked and waved. Every other seat on the plane was empty, giving us lots of room. The day's newspaper was laid out and waiting. Every town had its perks. In Dallas, the Justin Boot & Western Apparel store was opened for the Seahawks after hours. There were nightclub floor shows with stone crab in Miami and special treatment in restaurants. Tom Flores told us to look up an old friend's restaurant in Los Angeles. I don't remember how I got home. I *do* remember that the waiter never let me empty my margarita glass!

Once I missed the team bus in New York City. I flagged down a cab with an Iranian driver who spoke no English. He zoomed like a madman all around the city. I kept screaming at him, "New York Jets! New York Jets!" He kept jabbering into his radio and finally drove me to Kennedy International Airport. I leaped out and took another cab to Jet Stadium. When I arrived, a near riot was under way at the gate. It was the Jets' last season before they moved to the Meadowlands, and everyone wanted to get in, one last time. Burly cops were throwing people out, right and left. One fan would distract the guards while another tried to sneak in behind them. There were all sorts of lame stories, delivered in thick New York accents.

"My cousin has my ticket. He's inside, and if you let me get it, I'll prove it to you."

"Honest, I'm in K 28. Someone just stole my ticket."

"That's my girlfriend right there. See? Yeah. The one walking up the ramp. Hey, come back here! Dammit, she's got my ticket. Let me catch up to her!"

I worked my way through this rowdy crowd and approached the policeman. "Hi. I'm the Seattle Seahawks' doctor. I missed the bus, and I need to get in."

"Sure, go right on in." He looked at my open mouth and read my mind. "Listen, buddy. It's simple. No one from here would ever look me in the eye and actually talk with your accent. You couldn't possibly be lying." *My accent?* He opened the barbed-wire gate, and I went on in.

The week-to-week routine was simple. Sunday was game day. Afterwards, we got on the plane and headed home. Our injury clinic was at the Seahawk headquarters in Kirkland every Monday at 7:30 A.M. This early start gave us a jump on ordering emergency MRIs for hurt players. We could call around town and plead for emergency scanning before the clinics opened up for their regular patients. (Nowadays, with the new super-fast software, access to the scanner is no longer a problem.) In addition, the Seahawks got "block time" every Monday just to guarantee MRI access during the regular season. We would discover injuries on Monday morning that the players themselves didn't know they had on Sunday. It was amazing. The players' absolute focus on the game and the adrenaline rush combined to mask these injuries. During my years with the 'Hawks, at least eight players showed up with fractured bones or torn ligaments and had no idea that they'd sustained those injuries on Sunday. Sometime during the night, when the adrenaline wore off, something would start throbbing.

After we saw the game's injured players, Jimmy and I took the injury report up to the head coach. He had to know who was okay, who might need X-ray studies, who needed surgery, and who might not practice but would still be able to play on Sunday. This injury report was filed with the league office for publication and designated each player as out, doubtful, or probable. For me, the rest of Monday was spent trying to see my private patients while I caught up on what hadn't gotten done on Friday. I usually ran late on Mondays. Sometime during the day, the MRI radiologist would call and give his report. We always cautioned him to not report directly to the player. On the MRI, old injuries often don't disappear. For example, an old meniscus repair that was healed and stable might still look like a torn cartilage on an MRI. Therefore, the MRI needed to be interpreted by someone who knew the player's injury and surgical history. We went over the MRIs with the players ourselves to avoid any false alarms. If something bad cropped up on an MRI, it usually meant an addition to my surgical schedule that night.

Tuesday was the players' day off. They had to run on Monday mornings, loosening up to work out the stiffness and aches from Sunday's physical pounding. Then they studied game film with the coaches. This review could be brutal: missed assignments might be shown again and again in slow motion. After Sunday's game and the rehash on Monday, the players needed a physical and mental break. Jimmy set up Tuesday "night treatment" for those players with injuries for which extra therapy might be the difference in a quicker return. They still got their free day, but the night treatment allowed Jimmy to get a little extra work on their contusions, sprains, muscle spasms, and so forth. A lot of players responded to his hands-on, personal approach, and they would be able to play the next Sunday, whereas if they had been on another team without Jimmy's treatment, they would not.

Wednesday the players would put their pads back on. The coaches spent all of Tuesday studying the game films of the Seahawks' next opponent. Our strengths and their perceived weaknesses had been dissected. The offense practices next Sunday's game plan in a full-contact workout. As needed, portions of the summer camp's plays are resurrected each Wednesday and installed into the upcoming offensive scheme. That afternoon, I'd come over for the afternoon injury clinic. I'd check the progress of all our recent injuries and find out if there was anything new. Who was getting better? Who would be reclassified in that evening's injury report to the coach? Who could he count on next Sunday?

Thursday, it was the defense's turn. The second-string offense would wear the jersey numbers of our upcoming opponents, and they'd run plays out of that team's formations. It was a full-contact practice with pads and helmets. Once the defensive schemes were installed, we'd have a second afternoon injury clinic. Once again, anything new? Any vets with an ailing, arthritic knee? It was the last chance during the week for a shot. On the Seahawks, we rationed the cortisone. Our rule was, no more than three injections in an entire year. An old vet knew how to ration those shots, how to endure the pain when he had to and wait for the byes. I saw vets with bone-on-bone joints who played year after year and endured the pain. They had their pride, the game was all they knew, and the money was pretty darn good.

Friday came, and it was time for special teams. Rusty Tillman had them practice new strategies and work on disguising the old. He knew the other teams had been studying our game films as well. You could only do so much on special teams: kick off, punt, or return. You could return right, left, or up the middle. You had to identify the other team's speedsters and double up on them to keep them out of the play. One uncovered rocket could knock down your return guy the instant he caught the ball. If we didn't change, conceal, and adapt, we'd lose. One special-teams play could decide a game.

If we had a home game, the players took the enemy game films home that night to study. There would be a light workout on Saturday morning, then the players would report to our local hotel. If the game was away, the team flew out of Kirkland on Friday. We'd go to the enemy stadium on Saturday morning and then to a police-guarded bed check that night. It always amazed me how groupies looking for sex could somehow find their way onto the team floor—in any hotel, in any city. That's why we had guards. Sunday morning, it was time to strap it up for another game.

For the rookies, the middle of November brought mental misery. By this time of the year in high school and college, their season was over. In the pros, they still had six more games to go. Everything was faster and harder. Attrition began to rear its ugly head. The Kingdome playing surface was, in essence, a green rug over cement. By November, at least three quarters of the team was playing in pain. The constant pounding on the cement surface each Sunday sent throbbing waves up the players' shins. Their knees and low backs absorbed this pounding as well. Everything ached, especially at night. Half the team was on short bursts (three or four days' worth) of anti-inflammatory medication, taken to dull the pain. We'd start it on Sunday night when the pain was at its worst, and then we'd stop it by Friday. One quarter of the players would be nursing "mat burns." These were areas of partial or full-thickness skin abrasions where the artificial turf had ripped away skin. We covered these scabbed burns with salves, ointments, and an artificial skin to shield them for the next game. The cold whirlpool was cleaned and drained every night to eliminate the reddish-brown, scummy foam that congealed on the walls after treatment.

If we were in the hunt, this was the time to bear down. The wily old veteran, Reggie MacKenzie, would start the chant in the locker room. "Win in November, play in December. Win in November, play in December!" He was reminding the entire team, now in the depths of its pain and misery, to bear down and grind it out. The first playoff games come at the end of December. What we did in that four-week stretch of November determined whether or not we went on and played at the end of December. El-foldos typically occurred on young teams at this time. The squad could be 6–3 at the end of October and wind up 6–7 at the end of November! Little things could make the difference: a missed field goal, a dropped pass, or a fumbled handoff. One botched play due to inattention and loss of focus could lose a game.

When December came, we'd be dealing with one of three scenarios: we were in the thick of it, we *could* be in the thick of it (if another team lost), or we were out of it. Where we were was reflected in the medical practice. If we were out of it, no one played hurt. Nobody wanted an injection or cortisone shot. Team morale was low, and each day the training room was full of injured players covered with ice bags. Half of these players wouldn't even be there if we were in the thick of it. They'd be filled with a sense of urgency: "Doc, what can you do to get me out of here?" In either case, I'd spend the necessary time with them, explaining their treatment options and the medical risks or consequences of those options.

We always had a team Christmas party. In the early years, it was held in the Nordstroms' homes. Eventually, the event got to be too big, too much fuss, and too much risk. Serving alcohol to employees entails substantially more risk than just getting red wine on your carpet. The parties were therefore moved to a country club. Santa was there (with a real beard!), and all the Seahawk children got presents. There was good will and good cheer. Things eventually fell apart after the Behrings bought the team. In the last two years under Dennis Erickson, I couldn't bring myself to go. My sons had grown up, and there was no longer a sense of family at the parties.

The last game of the year was usually held in the Kingdome. Because the stadium contract with the Mariners gave them priority in September, we usually opened on the road. This invariably gave us a home game at the end of the season. The team's attitude was tempered by our position. Only once did we know before that last game whether or not we'd be in the playoffs. We thought our season was over in 1983 when we finished 9–7 with the last game on the road, but we wound up going to the AFC championship game. Then we finished 10–6 in 1985 and didn't make the playoffs. We destroyed the Broncos at home that year, but they went to the postseason, and we went home. Whenever we lost the last game of the season, it cast a terrible gloom over the organization for the upcoming off-season. In Tom Flores's last game, we lost on the road against Cleveland. The airplane trip home was like flying in a coffin. Everyone knew what was going to happen to Tom, and no one liked it.

Immediately after the last game, we'd start the release physicals in the locker room and finish them at headquarters the next morning. Any injury during the season had to be documented. Some players were going to need off-season surgery. Some would not be offered new contracts. Some would claim in the spring that they'd had an injury, and that the Seahawks were responsible for it. The release physical became a legal document. Our intention was to ensure that no one was released hurt. We also wanted to make sure no one demanded compensation for an injury when none had occurred. With each player's final signature acknowledging the completion of the release physical, the season would end with a whimper.

The end of practice, Seahawk headquarters, Kirkland, Washington. This headquarters, which was shepherded into completion by general manager Mike McCormack, became a model for many other NFL teams.

"Vitamin Iron"—the weight room.

The training room. Hall-of-Fame trainer Jimmy Whitesel (center) adjusting an orthotic insert in number 82 Paul Skansi's shoe.

Another day at the office. The medical staff tends to an injured Seahawk player.

During a game against the San Diego Chargers, the author (left) asks Seahawks linebacker Greg Gaines if he can extend his thumb. Dr. Scranton has just finished stapling shut a huge laceration on Gaines's hand without anesthesia.

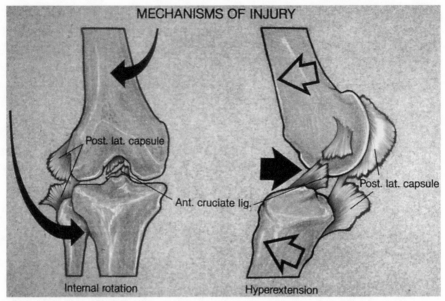

Biomedical Illustrations, Inc.

A diagrammatic illustration of how an anterior cruciate ligament (ACL) gets "blown." Hyperextension or violent rotation almost always tears more than one structure.

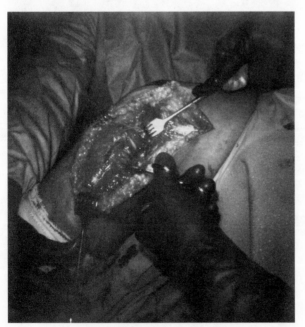

An actual intra-operative photograph of a shredded knee ligament reconstruction done the "old fashioned way." Two foot-long incisions were not uncommon in the early 1980s.

Author's Collection

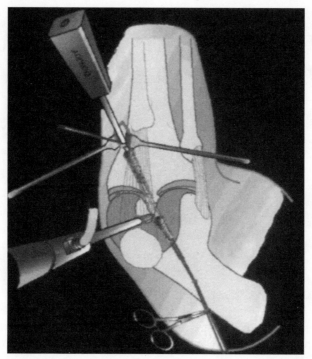

A diagrammatic illustration of how a torn knee ligament is repaired today. The arthroscopic procedure can be done as outpatient surgery in forty minutes.

All-Pro Curt Warner running wild in the Orange Bowl against the Miami Dolphins in 1983. Chuck Knox adjusted the offensive line gaps and the rest was history.

Robert "Papa Fig" Newton (78) and John Yarno (51). Even in repose on the bench, the intensity in their eyes is apparent.

The author (left) with NFL commissioner Paul Tagliabue in 1996 at the Kingdome, discussing the results of the shoe-turf safety studies.

Tom Flores

Player, coach, and general manager Tom Flores. On display are his four Super Bowl rings.

The author (right) with his former patient, Hall-of-Fame wide receiver and U.S. congressman Steve Largent at the Capitol dome in 1996.

SIX

The Making of a Winner:
Coaching and Playoff Fever

What makes the playoffs different from the regular season? If you think about it, we had the same teams, the same running and passing plays, and possibly even some of the same opponents we faced in the regular season. We also had the same banged-up players nursing the same injuries. Everything was the same, and yet, everything was different.

For starters, the hype made the playoffs different. You still have the same number of sports writers around at the end of the regular season, but half the league has been eliminated, so the reporters' focus narrows. If your team is in the playoffs, the local media become informational piranhas in a feeding frenzy. Community pride blossoms. Suddenly the governor of Washington is making political hay, talking about a "friendly little wager," say, a priceless item like the pride of Washington or a bushel of Washington apples against a crate of Florida oranges. The gadflies who have been harping and carping all year about the social consciousness and the waste of the country's economic resources on professional sports—they vanish faster than Houdini.

The players feel the pressure, but no more so than the coaches. After you've played 16 regular-season games, your playoff opponents are not going to see a lot of surprises. Installing a new offensive or defensive system for the playoffs would change the tempo of the team. By this point, the players are "clicking" in the rhythms and reacting instinctively to their respective offensive and defensive reads. Remember, if you have to think about what you're doing, it's already too late. What did Sam Merriman tell us? In a single pass-play defense, say second and eight, the middle linebacker may have four or five different coverages to drop into based on what the running back does—even before the ball's snapped. Zone, man, double, shadow the tight end—and these options might only apply for a two-back, "I" formation. The options could all change for a one-back formation or a back-in-motion. It would be wrong to install an entirely new system and confuse everyone.

Despite a fairly equitable distribution of talent throughout the league, certain coaches always seem to wind up in the playoffs. For example, success followed Chuck Knox from the Los Angeles Rams, to the Buffalo Bills, and then to Seattle. How about Dan Reeves? He made it to four Super Bowls in Denver. Then he went to the New York Giants, and bingo, they're in the playoffs. Now with Atlanta, Reeves took the Falcons to the Super Bowl, too. Look at Jimmy Johnson's career: an NCAA national championship and two Super Bowl wins in Dallas. After leaving Dallas because of a tiff with Jerry Jones, he took Miami to the playoffs several times. Bill Parcells? Wow! Two Super Bowl victories with the New York Giants. He goes to New England, and suddenly they're in the Super Bowl. When he can't get along with the owner, he goes back to New York to coach the Jets. Not since Namath have the Jets been anywhere, but Bill takes over, and suddenly they're back in the playoffs.

Having had some exposure to these coaches, I believe they share a common trait: they're control freaks. I don't mean this in a derogatory fashion. These men are meticulous in their preparation. They can recognize immediately whether or not someone can get the job done. If they perceive holes in their team, they will go out and find the necessary players to fill them. Conditioning is a must, and the players are driven to physical extremes before the first regular-season snap is ever taken. These coaches are disciplined. They minimize penalties from offsides, miscues, and dropped passes. If you have hardened, skilled players at every position, and they don't make mistakes, then you've increased your chances of making the playoffs. The players who fumble the ball, drop passes, and miss tackles are gone after the first year.

Once these coaches have assembled playoff-caliber teams, they must find a way to motivate the players in the postseason. By the time the coach makes it to the Super Bowl, there's another guy just like him running a team on the other side. By controlling every aspect of their players' professional lives, these coaches get the players to believe with every fiber of their bodies that their system and their coaches will not let them down. It's an ambivalent relationship, with the players fearing their disciplinarian coach and hating the physical pain they endure on his behalf, but also believing in him: "I'll bet that sonofabitch can actually pull it off and win us a big shiny diamond." In the heat of the battle, they'll walk through hell in a gasoline suit for him.

By playoff time, the smart coaches have already installed systems that work. Now that they're up to the next level, there's no reason to change the system. This is where the cliché comes in: "We'll dance with the one what brung us." They don't abandon what works. However, there's nothing wrong with disguising it maybe, just a little tinkering. On Chuck's desk was a copy of Sun Tzu's *The Art of War*. Sun Tzu said it best: "All warfare is based on deception. Hence, when able to attack, we must seem unable: when using our forces, we must seem inactive; when we are near, we must make the enemy believe we are far away; when we are far away, we must make him believe we are near. Hold out baits to entice the enemy. Feign disorder, and crush him." A smart coach will keep the same general coverage and not abandon his strengths. He will also attempt to hide from his opponent what his intentions are. He might run the same offense but change the O-line blocking splits.

Also, great coaches exploit their strengths. When you've got it, flaunt it! Make the enemy try to stop you. In Super Bowl XX, the Chicago Bears mauled the New England Patriots down in the Superdome by a score of 46–10. In short yardage, Mike Ditka had taken to putting in 300-pounder "Refrigerator" Perry to run the ball. When "The Fridge" was in the backfield, the Patriots knew he was going to get the ball; they just couldn't stop him. In Super Bowl XXIII, when the San Francisco 49ers played the Cincinnati Bengals, everyone knew that Joe Montana would try to get the ball to Jerry Rice. The key to stopping the 49ers was to stop Rice, but the Bengals couldn't.

In spite of the game plans, and in spite of the disguises, a football game still comes down to one thing: players who make plays. You can play the percentages, and you can use schemes that will increase the likelihood of mismatches, but in the end, the players have to execute. Two great football plays come to mind that illustrate this point. They were both showcased on *Monday Night Football,* and they both involved the Los Angeles Rams.

In the early eighties, the Rams were often in the thick of the playoff hunt. They had a superb defense, and they knew how to get points on the board. On *Monday Night Football*—with announcers Frank Gifford, Howard Cosell, and "Dandy" Don Meredith—the Rams were playing their chief rival, the San Francisco 49ers. For three quarters, the Ram DBs doubled up on Jerry

Rice and denied him the ball. This double team opened up the remainder of the 49ers' offense, but they just weren't able to exploit the opportunities. The Rams' defense was tenacious, and late in the third quarter, they faked a free-safety blitz, leading Montana to audible to Rice on a "go" route. The instant the ball was snapped, the blitzing free safety didn't blitz, but was already dropping back in front of Rice while the strong safety doubled on him deep. The ball arced over the field, and the free safety went up for the interception—exactly as planned, because their disguised free-safety blitz had really been a trap for Montana to throw long into double coverage. So the free was in perfect position, except that he bobbled the ball for an instant. And as it hung there, Rice reached over and took it out of the air. Behind him, the strong safety got wrong-footed, and in a slow-motion ballet, he tripped and fell to the turf. As he fell, he took out his own free safety, and their legs tangled, leaving them both to watch helplessly as Rice walked untouched into the end zone. *Players* make plays.

In another *Monday Night Football* game, the Los Angeles Rams were playing the Seahawks at the Kingdome. The Rams were basically kicking the crap out of us. They had a three-man front with four very active linebackers. They were totally stuffing our offense. Nevertheless, the game was still close in the third quarter because our special teams had been giving us great field positions and keeping the Rams deep in their own territory. We were driving with the ball on their 20-yard line. "Mudbone" Dave Krieg had taken a snap. Almost immediately, a pair of dogging linebackers were in his face. As he frantically rolled away, trying to escape, one of them swatted the ball out of his hands. It careened crazily across the turf, and, five yards away, amazingly bounced right back up into Davey Krieg's hands. He scrambled sideways to the right, spotted an open man, and threw a touchdown. Several years later, ABC had a call-in on *Monday Night Football* to recognize the most spectacular offensive play in their 25 years of telecasting. That play was voted the best.

"Win in November, play in December." Reggie MacKenzie's chant still echoes in my mind. For a team that had never been in the playoffs, our first trip in 1983 was an adventure. In that year's final regular-season game, the New York Giants scored the go-ahead touchdown against us, and it looked like we would finish a respectable 8–8 in Chuck's first year as head coach. And then we noticed a little yellow flag on the ground. "Holding against the offense, 15 yards. The penalty is accepted." We won the game, and instead finished 9–7; tying the Broncos' record. We were both wild-card playoff teams, but our better record in the AFC meant that Denver had to come to us.

Generally speaking, a team that has never been to the playoffs is usually doomed, but our coach, Chuck Knox, was no stranger to the postseason. When he coached the Rams against the Minnesota Vikings, he was one blown call away from being in the Super Bowl. The playoffs were where he excelled as a coach. The city of Seattle immediately went wild.

When I walked into the Kingdome training room that playoff day, I was struck by the fact that everyone knew we were going to win. No one said anything—there was just an air of confidence. I don't believe that a single player in that locker room doubted for an instant that we would win. They believed in the coaches' game plan, and they believed in the old vets who'd been brought in to help. Chuck had drafted Curt Warner, benched Jim Zorn, and then said Dave Krieg was the man to take the team to the Promised Land. By God, here we were! We went out and creamed the Broncos 31–7.

Injuries weren't a factor. When you're on an emotional roll, you feel immortal. Next it was off to Miami. The team wasn't feeling any pressure. When no one expects you to win, you have nothing to lose. Miami's record was 13–3, the best in the AFC. Our chartered Eastern Airlines L10-11 had mechanical problems, and we didn't arrive in Miami until 4 A.M. Former astronaut and president of Eastern Airlines, Frank Borman, called personally to apologize. No problem—we weren't supposed to win anyway. What's a little jet lag? The press had gone ga-ga over coach Shula's rookie sensation, Dan Marino. The media asked, "Dan, who would you rather play next after the Seahawks? The Steelers? Buffalo?"

Since we had nothing to lose, we didn't. Chuck adjusted the O-line splits, played the percentages, and the players made the plays. In the end, the Dolphins crowded the line to stop Warner and to sack Krieg. That left Largent one on one, and he came through. When the final gun sounded, we had won 27–20. I found myself on the sidelines screaming and hugging the Seahawk owners, Jimmy, players, and the water boy. We drank all of the plane's champagne before we'd finished taxiing on the tarmac for takeoff. When we arrived home at 1 A.M., several thousand fans were at the airport to greet us. They demanded and got a speech from Chuck. He could have run that day for mayor of Seattle, governor of the state, or the U.S. Senate, and he would have won by a landslide.

Only now, going to the AFC championship, did the Seahawks start to feel the pressure. It settled in like a silent fog. Everything became a crisis. We were one win away from the Super Bowl. From a medical standpoint, things became tricky. I was still bound by my Hippocratic oath, but Hippocrates was never in the playoffs! How does blocking a player with Marcaine so he can practice fit into the equation? That year, each Seahawk player had already earned $37,000 in bonus money and many were now getting commercial opportunities. To keep earning the bonus money and keep getting endorsement offers, a player wanted to avoid injury—never mind the fierce sense of team pride and the desire to win. For the players, there was no ethical quandary about receiving a shot for practice. "You gotta do whatever it takes to keep me in, Doc."

The media pressure was mounting, too. Despite having an unlisted number, I would get calls at home for interviews. I had to politely remind callers that I didn't do interviews. The players, of course, were besieged. Everyone's a star come playoff time. A no-name rookie free agent would look up from his locker and suddenly see ten faces with lights, cameras, and recorders.

"If you were a tree, what kind of tree would you be?"

"Say what?"

"When you bobbled that pass before you caught it, what was going through your mind?

"Huh?"

"What do you think your old midget-league football buddies think of you now, one game away from the Super Bowl?"

As I drove in for injury clinic, I saw uniformed strangers checking credentials at camp. Our head of security told me we needed more guards. Fresh-painted signs were posted directing hangers-on and the press to their designated interview areas. Our entourage was now so large that we needed two chartered planes for the flight to Los Angeles. We arrived and took chartered buses with a police escort to the Century Plaza Hotel.

A team can ride on emotional waves into the playoffs but eventually the wave will break unless the team has the maturity and confidence to rise to the next level. When you look back at the New England Patriots in Super Bowl XX, you see what I mean. They went from a wild card with nothing to lose to the Super Bowl and then finally choked. The Denver Broncos and the Minnesota Vikings each went time and time again to the Super Bowl—

only to fold. The pressure is incredible. When the Seahawks played the Los Angeles Raiders in the Coliseum for the AFC championship, we were at the height of an emotional wave. We had beaten the Raiders twice during the regular season. They had been to the playoffs many times, however, and we had not. They were accustomed to the media hype and the pressure. Our emotional wave crashed down on us.

When I walked into the Coliseum training room, I knew immediately that we were going to lose the game. Tension filled the room. A skinny, balding man was running around giving out "wicker water." How he ever got past security and into our locker room, I'll never know. He claimed this water was holy and had mystical healing powers. He carried a letter purported to be from President Reagan thanking him for the water's role in helping him recover from his gunshot wounds. When I saw the players running to this charlatan, looking for a magic cure-all, I knew that they'd stopped believing in themselves. We went out, and the Raiders killed us. Absolutely nothing worked: we dropped passes, muffed handouts, and made multiple miscues. Curt's ribs were broken, and Dave Krieg was repeatedly sacked. The only solace came from our center, Blair Bush. He'd been with Cincinnati when they lost Super Bowl XVI to the 49ers. He said, "Doc, if you think this is bad, imagine what it's like to lose a Super Bowl." The Raiders went on to win the Super Bowl, walloping the Washington Redskins. And just like every other year, whether we were in the playoffs or not, I wound up the season by performing the release physicals.

SEVEN

Catastrophic Injuries and the Toughest Players I've Ever Known

Injuries are a part of life in professional football. Each of the 11 men on each side of the ball is likely, even expected, to hit one or more opponents every time the ball is snapped. This type of contact is forbidden in most other sports.

In American football, the intent of each offensive play is for everyone (except the quarterback) to hit, knock down, or temporarily remove from play each member of the defensive team. The rules of contact are fairly simple: almost any hit from the front is legal. A few exceptions are subject to interpretation by the referee. For example, a player may not grab an opponent's face mask for any reason. If he does so accidentally, he commits an "inadvertent face mask" violation, resulting in a loss of down and a five-yard penalty. Intentional grasping of the face mask, wherein the player is dragged to the ground, constitutes a flagrant personal foul with a 15-yard penalty. Grabbing and yanking the face mask is dangerous because the player might get his neck vertebrae dislocated or broken and suffer paralysis. The players know this, and in my experience, intentional face-mask violations are rare.

The face-mask penalties I've seen usually involve a ball carrier and a defensive player trying to make a desperation tackle. As his one hand slips off a shoulder or hip pad, the other clutches the top of the helmet, slipping down until the tackler's fingers instinctively grasp the face mask. Although he isn't trying to grab the face mask, once he does, he can't let go. "Intentional face mask—15-yard penalty." The only really flagrant face-mask foul I witnessed came on a kickoff when our defensive back, number 44 John Harris, was pulled down by the face mask from behind by a Raider in a game at the Los Angeles Coliseum. The Raider then reached in and tried to gouge out John's eyes. The referees missed the foul and there were no penalty flags.

The rules of football also discourage certain types of contact involving a player's head. For example, a forearm shiver by a defensive back to the head or neck of a crossing wide receiver constitutes a flagrant foul. A spear by the helmet of either a defensive or offensive player is also considered a foul. Spearing—using the helmet as a projectile weapon—can be dangerous to both the spearer and spearee. The spearer may suffer unconsciousness with a concussion or serious neck injury. Central cord contusions, fractures, or dislocations with quadriplegia are possible results of spearing. Remember when Dennis Byrd of the New York Jets inadvertently speared his own teammate as they both blitzed the quarterback? He was paralyzed on the field. The spearee, however, is much more likely to suffer injury: unconsciousness, neck injury, a broken jaw, broken ribs, broken bones, or ligament damage. The retired linebacker David Megessey wrote about the cumulative effects of spearing he experienced while at Syracuse University and later in St. Louis as a member of the Cardinals in his book, *Not in Their League*.

Some forms of contact with the helmet are legal. For example, if the defensive player bursts through the line and makes a clean tackle and happens to smash helmets with the ball carrier, that's a legal hit. Legal, that is, unless it's the quarterback. The negative press on the epidemic of quarterback concussions and injuries has led referees to watch very closely for this type of contact. The quarterback's head is out of bounds. A defender will be assessed a fifteen-yard personal foul if he gives even a remote appearance of head-hunting against the quarterback.

The rules vary regarding contact with a player's legs. For example, during kickoffs or punts, the "crack-back block"—hitting an opponent below the waist from behind—is illegal. If a special-teams player is running all out and is suddenly blindsided in such a way that his legs are taken out, he's at high risk for catastrophic leg injury: a broken femur, tibia, dislocated knee, or torn ligaments. Similarly, offensive linemen are not supposed to hit defensive linemen at their knees. This is called clipping and warrants a personal foul with a 15-yard penalty. Picture an end-around sweep to the right. The right offensive tackle may try to knock down the defensive end and then quickly spin and dive into the legs of the pursuing nose tackle to knock him off his feet. If the offensive tackle succeeds, he puts two people on the ground and helps clear the right side of the field for the running back on the sweep. But if that offensive tackle either inadvertently or intentionally hits the nose tackle at the lateral knee joint, he can do more than put him on the ground—he can tear up his knee joint and end his career. When referees see an inadvertent clip, they'll call it and usually issue a warning. If they see what they believe is intentional clipping, they'll assess a 15-yard penalty and eject the player.

Chop blocking, a variation of clipping, also warrants a 15-yard penalty and ejection. Chop blocking involves one player driving into and standing up an opponent while his teammate cuts the opponent's knees. The helpless opponent can wind up with a complete knee blowout unless he manages to get off his legs. In addition to the ejection, the commissioner's office might fine the offensive lineman after reviewing the game films.

And the guy who's carrying the ball? His legs are "legal." If you're a 190-pound defensive back, and you have 250 pounds of fullback coming at you with the ball, you can dive straight at his legs to take him out. Whether your arms, shoulders, or helmet hits his legs is immaterial.

To avoid getting hurt by these leg shots in the NFL, you must have quick feet. Remember the combine physicals? One of the most sought-after criteria is quick feet. If a player's feet are planted, his legs are vulnerable to a blow. In a pileup or even in the open field, if a player plants his foot, it's an invitation to a knee blowout. The good running backs are gliders or darters. Even if he can't see it, a good running back can sense a coming blow and get off his feet. If his foot isn't planted, he may get a bruise, but no major injury. A standard cliché in football is that "the ball attracts a lot of attention." Great running backs such as Walter Payton, Billy Sims, and Tony Dorsett attracted a whole bunch of attention over the years. Virtually every defender tried to get at their legs to knock them down, but their quick feet forced a miss or glancing blow and saved their knees. Only when Tony Dorsett was in the last year of his career and had lost a step did someone hit him wrong and blow out his knee. Curt Warner was another great back, but his knee injury wasn't the result of player contact—his cleats caught on the Astroturf. He was betrayed by his equipment and the playing surface.

In spite of the protective equipment—the best that money and technology can provide—and in spite of the protective rules and referees, injuries still occur. Many of these injuries would be disabling to the average worker, but for an NFL player, such injuries might result in only a slight loss of practice time. A hip pointer is a good example. During a tackle, let's say an opponent's helmet strikes a Seahawk player's iliac wing of the pelvis, producing a severe hemorrhage and a chip fracture off the bone. This painful injury would probably result in at least three months loss of work for an ordinary person. In the NFL, however, a hip pointer would result in the loss of practice time only.

Prior to the next game, the injured player would come into our treatment room at the stadium immediately after a light, pre-game warmup. After administering a sterile Betadine scrub over the pointer, I would inject between 10 and 25 cc's of 0.25% Marcaine with Epinephrine into the center of this painful hemorrhagic bone bruise. Marcaine is the block of choice because it will generally last for up to four hours—enough time to get that player through the game. Epinephrine is used because it constricts the blood vessels and prolongs the block. I make these injections very carefully, repeatedly aspirating on the needle as I work the Marcaine anesthetic around. A lot of Marcaine injected directly into a blood vessel can cause cardiac ventricular fibrillation and death. After the block is completed, the player will run around and jump up and down to see if the block has been successful. If he still feels pain, more block! If the block works, Jimmy would then put a giant felt doughnut pad over the player's hip pointer. This pad would then be covered by a fiberglass-formed cup, which is taped into place. Over that goes the player's regulation hip pad. With a successful block and this extra protection, the player should be effective on the field during the entire game. After the game and a shower, we'll put a giant ice bag onto his iliac crest. A good block is just now starting to wear off. An ineffective block wears off earlier and usually means that the player plays the fourth quarter in pain. Frequently the adrenaline rush of competition is so strong that the players don't notice the block is wearing off. The pain is usually so bad after the game that the player will need narcotics like Vicodin or Percocet for pain control that night. This process is repeated each week until the pointer heals or the season ends.

Throughout the season, these Marcaine blocks were judiciously applied to many body parts of many players. The players were always told of the risks, and they were also told that they didn't have to receive the blocks. But the players, though they hated the blocks, invariably requested them.

All the players in the NFL understood that playing with pain is part of the professional game. A game-day check, a starting spot on the roster, playoff hopes, and professional pride were factors that figured into the decision. When the team was completely out of the playoff picture, very few players took a block.

These blocks were given for painful contusions, bruised or cracked ribs, intercostal muscle tears, fractured or dislocated fingers, hip pointers, and isolated shin contusions resulting from a leg whip. The players trusted me to decide what could be blocked without risk and what could not. Most NFL physicians would never block a player just so he could practice, and we never blocked a joint or shot up a muscle pull. Injecting anesthetic into the knee or an ankle risked permanent injury and constituted negligent malpractice. The only time I ever blocked a player for a practice was when we made the playoffs, and the player and coaches needed to know if that linebacker could function with a block in a game situation.

Injuries are unpredictable. Catastrophic injuries can sometimes be overcome, and smaller injuries can sometimes end careers. Something as simple as a "turf toe" might seem an innocuous injury, especially compared to a bleeding contusion and pelvic iliac chip fracture, but in some cases, a turf toe has proven to be a catastrophic, career-ending injury. An inferior orbit fracture in a wide receiver can lead to double vision. If poorly corrected surgically, such an injury would spell the end of that receiver's career. During two-a-days at the St. Louis Cardinals' summer camp, a player once dropped dead on the sidelines from a cardiac arrhythmia. The New England Patriots' Darryl Stingley was rendered permanently quadriplegic by a helmet-to-Helmet blow from Jack "The Assassin" Tatum. Football injuries range in severity from simple time-loss, to career-threatening, career-ending, or life-threatening injuries.

In the following pages, I've interviewed many players who experienced and overcame such injuries. These interviews will give you a firsthand sense of the pain these players suffered. In my opinion, they exhibited profound courage, perseverance, and high moral character in their comebacks. As you'll see, they are remarkable people with remarkable stories.

These individuals represent only a fraction of the players that I treated. While with the Seahawks, I performed, on average, 15 major operations per year. I successfully reconstructed the anterior cruciate ligament in the knees of about 38 NFL players, all of whom came back to play football. I've also dealt with unconsciousness, quadriplegia, a dislocated hip, three dislocated knees, fractured tibiae, fractured ankles, dislocated arches, and broken and dislocated toes.

Many of the players I contacted for this chapter were very grateful for the care they'd received, but declined interviews because they found it too painful to relive the catastrophic moment and the surgery and rehab that followed. The stories that you will read are special. I owe a debt of gratitude to these players for opening up their lives to share what it was like to look up from the Astroturf and see me looking down at them.

A common thread runs through this chapter—the trainer, Jimmy White-sel. If my surgical skill was the intellectual instrument of reconstruction, his thoughtful, hands-on, functional rehabilitation was the driving force, the motivation that transformed the reconstructed joint back into a functioning part. He turned the injured patient into a competitive football player who believed in himself. The interviews will therefore start at this fulcrum—the trainer.

JIMMY WHITESEL   May 13, 1999, Kirkland, Washington

Jimmy and I are in the den of his Kirkland home. It's like sitting in a time capsule—there are twenty-odd years of Seahawk memorabilia around us. Framed newspapers announce Seahawk championships. Signed game balls fill a shelf. Jerseys and signed photographs hang from the walls.

SCRANTON: "How did you become the Seahawks' head trainer?"

WHITESEL: "I went to Franklin Pierce High School in Tacoma, Washington. I was undersized, and not a very good athlete. I got injured several times, dislocating both my elbow and my shoulder. But because I liked sports so much, I wanted to be involved. So I wound up starting an athletic training program in high school. My senior year, our team was in the championship basketball series in Hec-Ed Pavillion at the University of Washington. I decided to walk down to the athletic training room and look up the head trainer, Bob Pedersen. I stuck out my hand and said, 'Mr. Pedersen, I'm

Jimmy Whitesel. I'm the student trainer at Franklin Pierce High School, and we're here in the state championships. I just wanted to introduce myself, because I'm coming here next year, and I'm going to be the best trainer you've ever had.' Pedersen sort of looked down at me and growled, "Well, if you're going to be my best, you'll be the first, because I've don't even have a program!' But he soon did, and I became the first student athletic trainer at the University of Washington. I graduated in 1966 and went on to get a master's degree in sports medicine under Dr. Jim Garrick. I became an assistant trainer at Washington State and then a head trainer at Seattle Pacific University. Finally, when the Seahawks were founded in 1976, I became the assistant trainer, and in 1983, I became head trainer."

SCRANTON: "What awards have you won during your career?"

WHITESEL: "I've won a lot, but many are awards that you don't win individually—you win them as a staff. I'm very proud of the people I've worked with here in Seattle over the years. Many of my assistant trainers are now head trainers across the country. In 1988, we were named NFL Athletic Trainer Staff of the Year at the annual Ed Block Courage Awards in Baltimore. My most prestigious individual honor came in 1998 when I was inducted into the National Athletic Trainer's Hall of Fame."

SCRANTON: "In the 23 years you were with the Seahawks, did you ever receive a game ball?"

WHITESEL: "Well here we are, sitting in a room full of game balls! And there's another room downstairs that has just as many. A few coaches gave game balls as a team award. Jack Patera was big on that. When we won a big game, he liked everyone to have the feeling that they were in some way a part of the team effort. I was proud of them, and it was a really good feeling, but they were team balls, not true game balls. Chuck Knox was the first coach who ever gave me a game ball for what I did on the field. You might remember it, because you got one, too. It was the season opener, a road game in Cincinnati. You know how hard it was to win an opener on the road. It was Curt's first game after his blown knee, and on top of that, it was 98 degrees on the field with 95% humidity. Well, we pre-hydrated the heck out of those players and altogether pushed on the field 158 gallons of Gatorade, water, and minerals. The heat was so devastating that by the fourth quarter almost one quarter of the Bengals couldn't play due to dehydration and muscle cramps. But our Hawks were still at full strength! Curt rushed for more than 100 yards, and we came from behind to win. Coaches like Chuck Knox and Tom Flores believed in rewarding outstanding individual effort. When you got an award, it really meant that you had contributed. It's different nowadays."

SCRANTON: "How did you plan for catastrophic injuries?"

WHITESEL: "Well, you can learn to tape ankles until you're blue in the face, and you can throw ice bags on anything that moves, but catastrophic injuries—that's what you have to prepare for during your entire life as a trainer. To a trainer, prevention is the greatest tool, and my work consisted of trying to prevent the catastrophic injuries that occur in the sport of football. But we also spent countless hours every year planning what we'd do in case of a catastrophic injury. That meant not only practicing with the equipment, but also actually bringing the EMS team in and practicing extrication, immobilization, and the transfer of an injured athlete. We all got pretty tired of loading each other onto that clamshell backboard!

"We had signs and hand signals to communicate from the site of the injury on the field to the people on the bench. The bench organization (the equipment personnel, assistant trainers, and so forth) knew where all of the medical equipment was, in what case or what trunk.

"If I put two hands on my chest, it meant we were in a crash-cart situation. If I had a hand behind my neck, it was a cervical type of situation—they'd come out with a Philadelphia collar. We extended our hands if we needed a long board, and we crossed our hands for the emergency kit. Doctor needs an X ray? Cross the arms. I would twirl my hands in the air to signal for the EMS unit (ambulance) to drive out and meet us on the field. We spent hours practicing these maneuvers. There were times when players had a concussion or something and they didn't need any help other than us bringing them to the sidelines. But we also had cases where players suffered quadriplegia or severe concussions and needed to be extricated carefully."

SCRANTON: "What do you mean by the term "extricated?"

WHITESEL: "A potentially serious injury to a player requires evaluation on the field, fitting him with a neck collar to protect his neck while his helmet is on, watching his airway, and then getting him safely off the field."

SCRANTON: "How many times did you have to take a player off the field on a backboard with a potentially catastrophic injury?"

WHITESEL: "Three times. When Al Davis got knocked out by a sideline sweep on the Raiders' side in the Kingdome, George was already there and we just sort of offered help. All three of our guys had major potential problems. There was the running back in the Miami Dolphins game, David Sims. Paul Johns, the wideout, hurt his neck in the Kingdome against the Chicago Bears. And then there was Tony Burse. For a while, two of those guys were temporarily quadriplegic, paralyzed on the field, and they could have had serious consequences if we mishandled their care. But each one of them is fine today, and that's because we took the extra time preparing and learning what to do. You were the one who warned us, 'The best intentions by people who aren't careful can lead to further neurological injury.' We never hurt anyone in the 23 years I was with the club, and I'm quite proud of it. We've had some serious cases and some funny cases. But no one ever suffered serious consequences from our treatment."

SCRANTON: "Funny cases?"

WHITESEL: "Like Alonzo Mitz. Remember in Kansas City? 'Zo goes down in this pileup, and when it clears, he's out there on the field, flopping around. You and I go out, and we just can't get him to hold still. Worse, we can't understand a word he's saying. 'Zo finally staggers up and wanders around, so we got him over to the sidelines to evaluate him. I remember you were screaming at him, 'Warrior, (that was his nickname then) what the hell's wrong?' But he'd only mumble something back. You kept yelling at him, and finally he held up his hand to stop your questions. He sat down on the bench, grasped his upper jaw with both hands, and with a crunch, 'Zo pulled his jaw and all his upper teeth back out straight. Doc, your eyes looked like they were going to pop out of your head! But Warrior didn't pay any attention to us. He put his mouthpiece back in and ran back out on the field. We never did get an eval.

SCRANTON: "Explain your principles in rehabilitating major knee reconstructions. How were you able to tailor the rehab to the injury and the player's position?"

WHITESEL: "Rehab means different things in different professions. In sports medicine, it means returning an athlete to function. And the demands for an NFL athlete are quite different from those of a middle-aged, weekend warrior. What I had to do was to put my mind to what each player did, the uniqueness of his activity, and the anticipated stress on the injured body part. It was different from one guy to the next. A lot of what I did back then equates to what we now call closed-chain rehab. Closed-chain rehab allows you to put the pedal to the metal, to take the athlete to the point where you're almost duplicating the tasks he performs on the field. Before anyone had even heard of closed-chain rehab, I was trying to set up programs that put players through the rigors of their actual jobs, that used circuits and things to really test their limbs and your repair, but not to excess.

"The process requires three things. First, the doctor had to give the player a good repair. Second, the player had to be dedicated, willing to be consistent in testing his limb and the repair. And finally, I had to have the right planned program that took the athlete sequentially through ever-increasing stress. If you didn't have all three components, nothing worked. Time pressures made rehab that much more difficult in the pros. With a recreational athlete, there's no rush. But a professional athlete needs to go on a different timetable and at a different level of performance. The whole team's future may depend on it."

SCRANTON: "How important was it for you to be in the operating room?"

WHITESEL: "In my younger years, I was in the OR a lot because, Lord knows, we had enough players who were in there all the time. That's where I learned where and when I could push or pull, because I knew exactly what kind of repair you had done and what the joint looked like. In recreational sports injuries, you see the isolated ACL tears, maybe a simple meniscus injury.

But in professional football, you saw combination injuries involving the ligaments, cartilage, and joint surfaces. You might see the ligament shredded, a cartilage pulverized, and maybe a section of the athlete's joint surface avulsed off. These injuries made for a very different type of rehab approach in these highly skilled athletes. But in the end, I didn't have to go to the OR as much. And that's because I knew how you operated, and I felt comfortable looking at your intra-operative photos and the videos. As long as I could still see what damage had occurred and what I needed to do, then I knew where I could push and where I had to unload and protect."

SCRANTON: "Did you have to deal with a lot of health-care fads?"

WHITESEL: "I received at least 30 letters a week from nutritionists, magnet people, and quacks wanting to show me special healing crystals and so forth. There are no quick fixes. The fact is, healing is healing in human beings. I had to place my hands on the players, work their joints and limbs to help them help themselves to get well. I had to give them a goal each day, something that they could attain, and then the next day I raised the goal. They loved me and they hated me, 'cause if I didn't spank them on the way, they wouldn't get well. Those gimmick things didn't work. . . . The only thing that worked was an athlete's ability to take what we gave him and push to a higher level. It was absolutely hands on, from the time I saw those patients in surgery to when I finally saw them take a snap and score a touchdown. One statement sums it up: "If you want to make footprints in the sands of time, wear work boots.' That's what those guys did in my training room—they wore work boots. We didn't rely on any shortcuts."

SCRANTON: "What was your most satisfying moment in the NFL?"

WHITSEL: "I've had some great moments, but hands down, winning in Miami was one of the best. It was electric. Even though we didn't get to the Super Bowl, we left Shula scratching his head and a lot of self-appointed East Coast sports experts wondering if they'd just had a bad dream or what. Winning that game with my family there was probably the most exciting thing I have ever felt. And coming back to Kirkland, watching the streets full of cheering people all along Lake Washington—that was special.

"Probably the most rewarding rehab out of the thousands I've done was Curt Warner. In 1983, he was Rookie of the Year, and actually, he was the guy who got us to that Miami game. The next year, he tore up his ACL. We worked as hard as we could for that entire year to bring him back. Keep in mind, Billy Sims in Detroit and that guy named Andrews down in Atlanta also blew out their knees. They never recovered, but *we* got Curt back. I mean, for a time, he actually lived with me. He wasn't married then, and after work we'd go swimming together at the Bellevue Athletic Club. As a matter of fact, I taught him to swim. He could kind of dog paddle, but he couldn't swim the way I wanted him to. So I shoved him off the deep end one day as we were walking in. He thrashed around so much, I'm sure it broke up some scar tissue! That really helped him. Curt did a fabulous rehabilitation with the type of reconstruction that was done at that time. It was 1984, and the surgery was all done with big incisions. He returned to the Seahawks that next year and rushed for more than 1000 yards. It was a great tribute to himself, and I'm proud to have been part of it. Curt always will be one of my best friends. He and his family have come to me for anything they needed in my clinic, and even if he came to my house (which he does) I still treat him as a brother."

SCRANTON: "What's the most difficult rehab you've ever done?"

WHITESEL: "I guess the problem nowadays is that these players don't want to get their treatment in-house. They want to do their own thing, or whatever thing their agents say they should do."

SCRANTON: "So free agency makes things different?"

WHITESEL: "*Everything* is different! Your club picks up some talented, high-priced free agent, but he's not part of the family. He has no loyalty. If he gets hurt, the first thing he'll do is jump on a plane and go see his agent. Then he goes to some surgeon of unknown competence who has no real knowledge of the player's physical athletic needs by position and who does some operation without any real communication with me on what he found and what he did. Finally, the player shows up and says, 'I'm ready to play football.' The track record of the guys who have left us to get their surgery elsewhere has not been good. That doesn't stop their agent's doctor from holding a press conference and letting everyone know how he's just saved so-and-so's career. But that's the difference between rehab of the 1980s and rehab of the 1990s. For a while I'd play devil's advocate with the players to try to get them back into our camp. But nowadays there's no recourse. It's not like family anymore. It's like you're just another worker in the rehab process. To me, that's not how you get people well. Like I said, you have to have the total package, all together."

SCRANTON: "Is there any particular case where you felt that you made a difference because you had a special understanding of a player's medical problem and the demands of his position?"

WHITESEL: "What made it possible for me to have an impact on our team was understanding each player's health history, his position, and how he responded to pain. One of the best examples I can think of was Jacob Green. Jacob was one of the NFL's best pass rushers in the 1980s. He came into camp one year and failed a test of shoulder strength that we do on every athlete. You guys immediately focused in on that, got X rays, and found some arthritis in his joint. Jacob was coming up for a new contract, and Mike McCormack and Chuck Knox all of a sudden got very interested in the results of this test. Historically, arthritis in the shoulder and a weak muscle could mean a player might wind up flunking your physical. So this test had big-time implications, both from the standpoint of his contract, as well as the defensive schemes that Chuck was planning. As I recall, we spent almost two hours arguing in Mike's office about all the what-ifs. Finally I just had to step forward and say, 'This is all bullshit!' I mean, here's this guy who, sure, maybe he doesn't pass a certain test. But functionally he can pass the big test. He can do what he has to do to play football. That shoulder X ray had nothing to do with his quickness off the line, his spin moves, his swims or cuts. Jacob Green could play football. He went on to play quite effectively for us for three more years in the NFL. Now he's up in the Ring of Honor."

SCRANTON: "In the early years, when 125 players would show up at summer camp in Cheney, what would you look for the tip-offs, that told you a particular guy could make it in the NFL?"

WHITESEL: "QABs. Quickness, agility, and balance. That's what separates a professional athlete from the rest. Heart, focus, and intensity are important too, but QABs win football games. You can even tell during the combines. You can see the athletic ability. I couldn't be a scout because I don't understand the position-specific things those guys are looking for in performance. But as far as physical ability, intensity, and focus—we saw it. Every summer in Cheney, there'd be, say, 80 to 100 players who would last until the first cut-down. And every year, my first assistant, John Kasik, and I used to formulate our final 45-man rosters before camp even started. It was a friendly wager: whoever had the most correct choices got a bottle of beer. Invariably, his choices were almost exactly the same as mine, because we knew who had the QABs. Within a week, you could pick the 50 guys from what was left of last year's team, half of your draft choices, and throw in maybe four or five poppers, you know, the guys who open the eyes of coaches. You could have cut training camp down to five days and moved back to Kirkland to start the real camp."

SCRANTON: "So speed has nothing to do with QABs."

WHITESEL: "Speed is only a part of quickness. Steve Largent was definitely not the fastest guy in the league. He ran maybe a 4.6 forty. But he had great QABs. He could put a guy on his ass right off the line of scrimmage, because the guy didn't know whether to look at his lower body or his upper body. Everything was going in different directions! He had the ability to separate himself from a defender who had far more speed, because he had QABs.

"Steve also had the absolute ability to focus. Chuck Knox liked to say he didn't care how intelligent somebody was; all he cared about was his ability to concentrate. I remember Largent would always go over to the stadium early, even before the team bus. He would walk the entire field himself, looking for any spot that might offer an advantage: a low spot here, a wet, soft spot in the grass there, or some spot where the artificial turf might have been worn. He had the whole thing committed to memory so that he could use those parts of the field to his advantage. He could make his move, and the defensive back might slip just a half a step, but that was all he needed."

JOHN YARNO   April 29, 1999, Bellevue, Washington

I'm in the showroom of Lexus of Bellevue with John Yarno. John was the Seahawks' center for six years. He's now a successful salesman for the Lexus dealership. John's brown hair is cut in a flattop. He wears a silk tie and cotton shirt. His collar button seems ready to pop from the pressure of his massive neck. John has mischievous blue-gray eyes and a quiet confidence. Unlike many of the players I interviewed, he was able to discuss his injuries in a matter-of-fact manner. For others, the memory was too painful.

SCRANTON: "Where were you born, where'd you go to school, and how'd you become a Seahawk?"

YARNO: "I was born in Spokane, Washington, on December 17, 1954. I went through the Catholic school system in Spokane—Sacred Heart Grade School, then Gonzaga Prep. My senior year I transferred to Ferris High School, and then I went to the University of Idaho on a football scholarship from 1973 through 1976. I was drafted by the Seahawks as a fourth-round pick in 1977."

SCRANTON: "What's your best sports memory?"

YARNO: "I could probably give you a top-ten list, but if I had to pick just one, it was the opening play of my senior year at Idaho. We were playing at Boise State, our big rival. It was one of those times you're in a zone. On the opening kickoff, I de-cleated three guys, knocked them practically out of their shoes, and my guy scored from 100 yards out. I led him into the end zone."

SCRANTON: "How about in the pros?"

YARNO: "There is one play that I'll never forget. It was 1978, and we were playing the Minnesota Vikings. We were on about the 15-yard line, going in. I don't know if it was second or third down, but our offensive coordinator called a draw play up the middle. In that draw play, I was supposed to block the middle linebacker. Problem was, they had two backers stacked over the guards, and they ran what we call an X-blitz, where one backer would come from one direction, and the other one would cut off his back and through the middle. So there were two guys coming and only one blocker—me. So I blocked them both. I knocked one guy down, spun, and then cut the second guy in the hole. David Sims walked into the end zone. I will never forget Howard Mudd (the offensive line coach) saying it was the finest play he'd ever seen an offensive lineman make."

SCRANTON: "How about injuries? What motivated you when you were hurt?"

YARNO: "Pierce, there are two expressions we've always had in the NFL. One was, 'Get hurt, lose your job!' Because if you're not on the field, somebody else is, and at that level, he's probably a pretty good athlete. Chances are, if the team has some success with the other guy in the lineup, you may never get to play again. Cal Ripken's streak started because some guy just took a day off. And more than 2000 games later, that guy's never gotten back onto the field in Baltimore. The other expression is, 'You can't make the club in the tub.' If you're not on that field every day and on the practice film the coaches study at night, then you're not in their minds. I mean, it's extremely competitive. It's very difficult. When I was with the Hawks, we'd take maybe 125 guys into summer camp for 48 jobs. If somebody went down, it was like, 'Drag that carcass off the field or move the drill, and let's go!' So it was a very violent lifestyle. But I would do the whole thing again in a heartbeat. I have no remorse about that."

SCRANTON: "How'd you make the Seahawks' team?

YARNO: "I had to prove that I could play at that level. I was coming out of the University of Idaho, which is a smaller college, and I was playing against guys from Nebraska, Notre Dame, and UCLA. I remember I got my first start in 1978 in a preseason game against the Chicago Bears. I was blocking downfield on a sprint draw, and Sherman Smith cut off my block. The safety came up to tackle him. He got his arms around Sherman, but Sherman just blew through it, and the guy's legs kind of went out and whipped around, and he got me right on the outside of the left knee. I go down, right? Then I got back up, got back into the huddle, and I continued through that series. When I came off to the sidelines, they started messing with my knee and telling me, 'You know, you've got to sit!' They had to restrain me on the sidelines. Finally I went in for another series. When I came out again, they made me sit on the bench, and I was a madman. I knew that this was my opportunity. I wasn't going to let them take me out. When we got done with the game, the doctor said I had a tear of the medial collateral ligament in the left knee. The next morning, I'm back in Seattle, reading the newspaper about how I'm out for six weeks! (John flashed a grin.) I missed one practice. I said to the trainers, 'Screw it, I'm playing! Do what you have to do—tape it, brace it, shoot it—I don't care. But I'm not missing my opportunity, because this is *my* chance.'"

SCRANTON: "What would you tell today's players?"

YARNO: "I've always felt that professional football is *not* about the money. It's about competing at an extremely high level. A player should enjoy it while he has the chance, because you never know when that chance will be taken away. It can end so quickly. Every guy I've ever talked to was stunned when he left the league, because he thought he still had at least two good years left in him. But your skills erode without your knowledge. You can't see it, but it happens.

"The salaries these guys are making now . . . You know, I'm pretty sure my total earnings in six years in the NFL don't add up to one year's minimum base salary for a free-agent rookie. If these guys do some decent planning with their money, they should be able to make the transition to real life fairly easily. There are lessons that I've taken from athletes and applied to the business world, raising a family, life—the things I do. I learned about teamwork and discipline in the NFL and it's served me well. You know, we all played hurt, and you carry into each year the previous season's injuries. It's like every year they take a little piece of you. Every campaign in the NFL, there is a 100% injury rate. Everyone gets hurt to some extent at some time, and every year you just stack that on. It's really a battle of attrition that wears you down over time.

"Remember that Dallas Cowboys game in 1980 on Thanksgiving Day? We went through a three-game stretch where we played Oakland on *Monday Night Football,* the Broncos on the road six days later on Sunday, then Dallas on the road that Thursday, Thanksgiving Day. Three games in ten days—talk about the battle of attrition and stacking up of injuries. You remember how we kidded around, offering to buy you a Mexican bandit's bandolier to carry all your hypodermic syringes full of juice? I think there was between six and 10 needles lined up on a tray, with player's names taped to each syringe. The biggest one had my name on it! I think that's where I gave you the nickname of Macho Doc!"

SCRANTON: "Tell me about your knee. What happened and how did you deal with it?"

YARNO: "Growing up, I don't think I ever missed a practice. I know I never missed a game. Coming into the NFL and winning the starting job in my second season, I felt that I was pretty invincible, that I would never get hurt. You learn pretty quickly in the NFL that it's not that way. My knee injury came in the thirteenth game of the 1978 season, my first year as a starter with the Seahawks.

"We were in Oakland, playing the Raiders. It was the first play of the second half, and we were running a tight-end screen towards the left, close to the sidelines. I was going against a guy named Mike McCoy who'd played at Notre Dame. He was a nose tackle. I gave him the slip, you know, the oh-shit block, and then I released and slipped into the screen. The force man came up, I read the force, and I knocked him down. I planted one foot to start to turn upfield to look for a second block. I had hit the force guy so well that the tight end decided to cut outside of me, towards the guy who I'd knocked backwards, because I'd totally knocked him out of the play. In the meantime, Mike McCoy smelled a rat, and he was chasing the play now. (Laughter.) McCoy is 6′5″, 285 pounds—a huge man—and he tried (more laughter) to jump over me to get at the tight end who was cutting outside my block to go up the sidelines. McCoy actually got up over my shoulder. My left foot was planted. I was turning back to the inside middle, and McCoy was up on top of me when he finally ran out of gas. I had 300 pounds or so on top of my right ear, and then I started going down, down. And then my knee went 'pop, pop.'

"My foot was level with my hip joint, and I was looking at my cleats, lying on the ground. I thought for a moment, 'There's obviously something wrong with this picture.' I had never been in a hospital in my life. I had never been hurt. I rolled over onto my stomach, and I was about 10 yards from the sidelines. I had never been carried off the field. I tried to crawl to the sidelines. I hand-over-handed it in the grass at Oakland Alameda County Stadium, and I was grabbing the grass and trying to drag myself so I wouldn't be carried off the field. The trainers saw what had happened, and it was fairly evident to them that I had practically torn the bottom half of my leg off. I got about halfway to the sidelines before they were on top of me. They told me to lie down, roll over, and stop. Then they picked me up. Norm Evans, who was our captain and this tremendous Christian gentleman, got an absolute earful of obscenities as they carried me off the field. I sat down on the bench, and I remember crying. I knew that I had been hurt pretty badly. I was probably in some sort of shock. I refused to look at the knee.

"I just kept my head back, and Walter Krengel, your partner, who was the orthopedic surgeon covering that game, took my knee and did the test where they move it from side to side to check the medial collateral ligament. My knee just opened up like a gate. Then he planted my foot on the turf to check the anterior cruciate ligament. When he pulled it forward, there must have been six inches of play. He patted me on the shoulder and said, 'You're done.' They gave me crutches to get back to the locker room from the bench area. They didn't have the little carts like they do now. I remember stopping at the top of the ramp, just before I lost sight of the field. We ended up winning the game, you know. We won four consecutive games against the Raiders in 1978 and 1979. It was a big deal! I remember that feeling of despair, that I was out of the action, even though I could still see it going on behind me. I went to the locker room, dressed alone, showered alone. I learned that when you're hurt, it's like you have a disease, and you're contagious. Everybody on the team just kind of stays away from you, like you don't exist."

SCRANTON: "What did you go through during rehab?"

YARNO: "Well, you know, Doc, this was back in 1978. They cut back then. It wasn't like the arthroscopic surgery of today. (Yarno grins.) None of that sissy surgery! They opened it on both sides, so I had these two incisions about eight inches to a foot long. The anterior cruciate ligament was torn off the bone, so they drilled into the bone and screwed it back. I guess that was good, because at that time they didn't have to reconstruct it, and the attempts weren't working out so well back then. The medial collateral ligament was ripped in half, and they sutured it back together. I wound up in a cast all the way up to my hip for six or eight weeks, totally immobilized. They didn't even have hinge casts back then. When the cast came off, my leg looked like a noodle. I mean, it was *totally* atrophied. My knee joint was actually bigger than the muscles, and it looked awful. The first thing I remember was I had to get my motion back. That was a long and painful process of breaking up what they called adhesions. I'd have to get in a warm tub and work the knee down until it would pop, and then something would give, and I could maybe move it a little more until the next struggle for even more motion. There were countless isometric leg lifts, you know, with just a weight on my ankle. One thing I *did* get out of this was I became a big reader. It was so boring, sitting in the training room week after week, that I started to read books while I was going through all the heat and massage and stuff. I would lie there for hours, and I read a ton of books.

"Once I regained the motion, it was a matter of trying to build the muscles back up. Jimmy and the staff at the Seahawks kept working me with the Cybex machine. This involved a great deal of pain and frustration, because there was a delicate balance—if you don't push, you go nowhere; if you go too fast, you risk a setback that might take weeks to overcome. And I had a couple of very frustrating setbacks. I was injured in November. By the time I got to the May mini-camp, I could run somewhat. I did a lot of swimming. I was not anywhere near healed. They held me out of two-a-days when we went back to Cheney. In fact, I didn't practice for the first couple of weeks. There were times when I felt like they were using me as a guinea pig. They'd say, 'Here John, go do this,' and I'd go run into a wall or whatever they asked me to do (Yarno laughs.) You remember the hill, Doc?" (*It was a 45-degree hill, 15 yards long, between two different levels of playing fields at Cheney.*) I got pretty good at that hill. There was a stairway up it, and then there was *my* path down it. As the month went by, the path got deeper and wider, and pretty soon, my path down was more like a four-lane highway. That summer was a lot of pain and hard work. I didn't play in the first two preseason games, and then in the third game, I think I played in two series. And I was so happy to be able to get back on the field, to do what I loved so much, that I didn't care what else happened. In the last preseason game, I think I played a half. Then I played every offensive down that year."

SCRANTON: "And for four more years after that."

YARNO: "Actually, five, counting the USFL. I'd been in the hospital, and they'd said, 'You may never play again.' But the following year, 1979, I played every single offensive down. It was almost like something that I had to prove, and that the coaches wanted me to prove as well. There was this one game where I was extremely ill. I was throwing up on the sidelines. We were ahead by 20 in Kansas City on a freezing cold day, and they wouldn't pull me out of the game. At the time, I was really mad. I thought, 'God, give me a break. It's November, I've gone through this season, I've rehabbed the knee, and I'm sicker than a dog!' But I played the whole game, and now it's something I'm very proud of, coming off a 'triad injury' to my knee.

"I don't think I even lost a step. There were other guys I knew who were always affected, but I felt like my skills eventually came back at 100%. But then, in the fifteenth game in 1980, I tore up my other knee, and from that point on, I was never the same. I had some pretty bad joint damage with that one. But playing in the NFL was a great time. No regrets."

GREG GAINES   April 17, 1999, San Diego, California

Greg Gaines was the toughest man I've ever met. Hands down, no one has come close. In fact, when I contacted former Seahawks regarding interviews for the toughest 'Hawks, every one of them asked if Gaines was going to be included. Greg has agreed to let his medical history do his talking for him.

Greg Gaines was signed by Jack Patera as a free agent in 1980. He was an undersized defensive back-linebacker out of the University of Tennessee, 6'1" and 206 pounds wringing wet. They projected him at right outside linebacker. He had

Jimmy's QABs and predatory football instincts. Greg was always around the ball. If they called his number on an outside linebacker blitz, he was a ferocious pass rusher who'd do whatever it took to get there and put a hurt on that quarterback. Nevertheless, he was still undersized. During his prime, he played at about 225 pounds, and if the offense ran a sweep around his side, he just got creamed (though he never backed off the pulling guard's block).

To me, Greg exemplified the ferocious, hard-nosed NFL player who relishes contact, the rush of physically beating another team, all for the love of the game. He reveled in competition. Hurt or not, when it was time to strap 'em up and go, Greg was always ready. Today he's in player personnel for the San Diego Chargers.

Injury #1, 10/26/81: New York Jets, a late afternoon game in Jet Stadium. Greg blows out his knee on a special-teams kickoff. He tears the anterior cruciate ligament, partially tears the medial collateral ligament and the lateral capsule, and his tibial spine gouges a chunk out of his articular surface of the lateral femoral condyle. My partner, Dr. Walter Krengel, and I perform the surgery. We make two incisions, 6 and 8 inches long. It takes about two hours and 10 minutes. We place Greg in a long, padded, fiberglass cast, which was standard treatment at that time. He is so obsessed with recovering function and working the leg that he destroys four casts in six weeks by trying to walk on and use the leg against medical advice. We send him a registered letter notifying him that he is noncompliant.

In the next phase of rehab, Greg is so gung-ho that he sustains a one-by-four-inch, second-degree burn on his entire anterior shin when he places steaming hot packs on the knee to heat it up so he can loosen scar tissue and gain motion. As a result of the giant surgical incisions, some of the sensory nerves to his shin have been cut. His burn on the insensitive skin is so bad that we have a dermatologic consultation with Dr. Bernard Goffe. Prescription salves and antibiotics are prescribed.

Four months later, in the next phase of rehab, Gaines develops severe, bilateral shin splints while running gassers. He's been driving himself like a madman and now has swollen, pitting edema over excruciatingly painful shins. We take X rays and get a bone scan to rule out stress fractures. Cross-training, special orthotics, physical therapy, and anti-inflammatory medication are prescribed. Gaines goes to camp in Cheney that year. Not once does he ever back off. He makes the team.

Injury #2, 11/5/82: Greg avulses the great toenail during a regular-season game. He continues to play after taping the toenail in place himself at halftime. Back in Seattle, we see Greg in injury clinic. The ripped-off toenail bed is now infected. I remove it under local anesthesia and place him on antibiotics.

Injury #3, 9/25/83: Greg partially dislocates his right great toe while playing on Astroturf. X rays confirm that he does not have a fracture. We apply a steel-toed orthotic to the shoe and tape his toe protectively. He requests a block to play in games. He misses no playing time.

Injury #4, 12/29/84: Greg dislocates his right shoulder in our first wild-card playoff game on the road against Miami. I reduce the shoulder on the sidelines using a Kocher maneuver. He plays the rest of the game. Afterwards, we perform an examination under anesthesia as well as an arthrogram-CAT scan to determine the extent of damage. We inform Greg that he has an anterior capsular tear, but he lets us know it doesn't really matter at the moment, because he'll be playing against the Raiders in a shoulder harness. After that AFC championship game loss, he undergoes a modified Open Bankhart-Magnuson-Stack shoulder reconstruction. Within four months, Greg is back with full motion and bench pressing 300 pounds.

He also dislocated his right fifth finger that season and ruptured the ulnar collateral ligament at the proximal interphalangeal joint. He pulled the finger back into place himself and then had Jimmy "buddy-tape" it to his fourth finger. He played all season with the injury. The finger continued to be unstable after the season, so Greg has the ulnar collateral ligament reconstructed by a hand surgeon, Dr. Steven Fuhs.

Injury #5, 10/2/85: Greg fractures the metacarpal of the left hand. The hand is protectively casted with outside padding to make it legal during a game (so it can't be used as a weapon or club). The injury heals during the regular season. Greg misses no playing time.

Injury #6, 12/30/85: Greg has arthroscopic surgery at the end of the season on his right knee. Thickened scar tissue and a small tear of the cartilage are removed. Greg actually complained of this injury during summer camp's two-a-days, but he decided to hold off on surgery until the off-season. We also examine our old ACL reconstruction; it is rock solid.

Injury #7, 10/2/86: Greg ruptures the long head of his left biceps muscle during a tackle. He comes off the field for one play to find out what's wrong. We treat him nonoperatively, and he misses no playing time. To this day, he still has the balled-up muscle in his upper arm, a "Popeye" deformity.

Injury #8, 12/09/86: Greg suffers a severe wrist sprain, fracturing the ulnar styloid and disrupting the scapho-lunate ligament. His wrist is placed in a protective cast, and he plays the remainder of the season. He requires a ligament reconstruction in the off-season. He also plays the entire season with inflamed, chronically draining ingrown toenails. In the off-season, we cut right down to the bone on each border, removing the germinal bed that grows the nail. We can't convince him to wear looser shoes.

Injury #9, 7/21/88: Greg ruptures a lumbar disc in the low back during preseason weight training at the L5-S1 disc space. The injury requires an open laminotomy and disc excision for the ruptured disc. Greg plays the entire 1988 season without incident. He rips open his thumb down to the tendon at Jack Murphy Stadium against the Chargers. I staple it without an anesthetic on the sidelines, and he misses two plays.

The Seahawks released Greg in 1989 and he was picked up by the Kansas City Chiefs. Their doctor at that time was Dr. Howard Elfeld, who called me in disbelief about Greg's injuries. He played for the Chiefs that year, but then he ruptured another disc, which required a second laminotomy and discectomy. This last operation led to his retirement from the NFL.

Greg's hard-nosed play and his instincts for football didn't go unnoticed. When Chuck Knox left Seattle for the Los Angeles Rams, he picked up Greg as an "intern" coach in scouting and as an assistant linebacker coach. Greg's back continued to trouble him, and he underwent two attempted spine fusions, neither successful. He's now contemplating a third attempt—*after* the San Diego Chargers draft.

Before I hung up the phone, I asked Greg if he had any regrets about playing ball.

"Pearston (This is what Greg calls me—some inexplicable combination of thick Tennessee twang and his chronic mispronunciation of my name), I don't regret a day of it! In fact, Pearston, y'all jus' know, I'm still gonna' get that Super Bowl ring."

PAUL MOYER   April 22, 1999, Seattle, Washington

I interviewed Paul in my fourth-floor medical office. He was with the Seahawks for seven years, first as a backup, then as starting strong safety. He was also a special-teams player. He then spent five years as a defensive backs coach. At the time of this interview, he was 37 years old and running three separate businesses, including a successful evening sports talk show on KIRO radio. Over the years I've seen many of our retired Seahawks players whose faces show the tremendous stress of life in the NFL, but Paul looks as though he's hardly aged a month since I gave him his first Seahawks physical. He is trim, wearing pleated olive slacks, a black turtleneck sweater, and a casual brown Nordstrom's sports coat. He has an Etruscan-like nose and intense eyes.

SCRANTON: "Where'd you learn to play football?"

MOYER: "I grew up in a little suburb in Orange County, where I went to Villa Park High School. Then I went to Fullerton Junior College where I was an All-American junior college player. Since I did well, I went on to Arizona State. I got pretty discouraged there, and I wanted to quit. But my junior college coach, Hal Shierbeck, kept supporting me, so I stuck it out and had a great senior year. My best memory that senior year was the Fiesta Bowl against Oklahoma. I had 20 tackles! But I hurt so badly the next day that for the first time in my life, I literally could not get out of bed. I was that sore."

SCRANTON: "So then what happened? Were you drafted?"

MOYER: "Well, Doc, we liked to call it 'getting drafted in the thirteenth round.' You see, there were only 12 rounds back then. And when the draft was over, the phone started ringing off the hook. George Dyer was my defensive coordinator at Arizona State, and Chuck Knox had hired him up in Seattle. So all these teams were calling me, and finally George got through. He said, "Listen, we want you to come up here as a free agent.' I sort of hemmed and hawed and said, 'Well, you know, you'll have to talk to my agent.' But George says, 'Listen, Chuck Knox wants to talk to you.' So I hear a little rustling, and Chuck comes on the phone and says, 'Paul, you know we really wanted to draft you up here. But the way the picks went and all

. . . blah, blah, blah. You really fit into our needs, and like, hey, this is even better.' So I wound up saying yes, took my phone off the hook, and went to bed. Anyway, I found out two years later that George hadn't actually given the phone to Chuck Knox, but to Joe Vitt, the strength coach. They figured, how the heck would I know whom I was talking to? So I took their line of bull—hook, line, and sinker. They had a great laugh over that, I'm sure."

SCRANTON: "So here you come to Seattle, a long-shot free agent. How'd you get your chance?"

MOYER: "I was way down on the depth chart. I was behind Kenny Easley, Don Dufek, and another guy named Ken McAllister. But I understood from the get-go that if you left the ball on the ground, someone would pick it up and run with it. So I knew if I was going to make the team I would have to play hurt, hustle, do whatever it took. And that's how I got my shot in the NFL. I think Dufek's agent had him holding out over some contract issues. Then McAllister had a tragedy in his family, and he had to go back briefly for a funeral. So I got moved up in camp to second string, and I knew right then that I was going to play hurt if I had to, because no one was going to put me on the sidelines. When the final cuts were made, I made the team."

SCRANTON: "What was it like getting hurt, playing hurt, and having surgery as a football player?"

MOYER: "This is kind of weird, but I used to like the immediate pain. You know, a lot of people can't handle pain. I *liked* pain. When I broke my shoulder (scapula), it was like, 'Man, I can dish it out, and I can take it. I can do this!' I mean, it was strictly personal. Actually, Doc, I think I was pretty lucky injury-wise. In fact, I think you only got to operate on me three times: two on the shoulder and an ankle 'scope for spurs. You know how I played: I'd play all out. I'd come in fists flying, giving it my all. Sometimes my hands were so bruised and puffy, you couldn't even see the knuckles. It was almost a euphoric pain."

SCRANTON: "What'd you think about the medical care in the NFL? Be totally honest. What you say gets printed."

MOYER: "I think a lot of times the doctors and trainers were perceived as being a part of management. There were a lot of players who said, 'I don't trust them!' Well, I trusted you guys like you were a part of the family. I always had good experiences with our trainers and our rehab, as well as the surgeries. I didn't have any complaints. We trusted you, Doc, and not just as the orthopedic Doc. I mean, I came to you with, 'Hey, I've got a cold.' And I can remember you saying, 'Hey, I'm really not that kind of doctor.' And I said, 'Yeah, but I've got the cold, and I know you can help me out here.' That's the kind of trust we had in you."

SCRANTON: "What about The Hit, the one injury that no one on the team will ever forget?"

MOYER: "Oh yeah. It was in 1986, and we were playing the Broncos in the Kingdome. Orson Mobley ran what we call a 'hook and go,' or a 'stop and go.' I bit on John Elway's fake. I should have known better since I played against him in the Pac Ten when he was at Stanford, but I did bite on the fake, and I was coming up. Orson stopped, and then he was going. The good news was that I was always smart enough that if someone beat me, I was going to pull him down. So when I grabbed Orson, he grabbed me back, and you could say he sort of came up with his right knee. In fact, you could actually say that he kind of pinned my right testicle against my thigh! So I went down. I was hurting pretty badly. You and Jimmy got me off to the sidelines, and we weren't sure exactly how bad it was, and I was kind of on my knees, moaning. So John Kasey, our kicker, comes up and says, 'Hey, Paul, I think you've got blue balls. They're probably up inside. Why don't you jump off the bench a couple of times?' So I go and jump off the bench, and I'm about to throw up. Finally, you guys took me in at halftime, and the trainers put ice on them. They followed that with an extra-large soft cup, followed by a hard cup.

"So we went out and played the second half. I'm sick the entire time, but you know, I could play. Actually, I had a pretty good game, which was kind of weird. It all came down to focus, because I focus when I get injured.

After the game, I remember walking into the locker room, and I pulled down my pants, and at that point I started screaming. I said, 'Oh, my God!' My testicle was hanging down to my knee. It had completely ruptured. Then a funny thing happened. You guys just happened to see a urologist coming by, a friend of somebody's in the locker room. It was like a freak coincidence, totally out of the blue. So in walks this urologist (Dr. Robert Calhoun), and real casual, like this happens to him every day, he says, 'Oh yeah, it looks like a ruptured testicle.' And all the players are coming up and saying, 'Oh my God, look at that!'

"So we go to the hospital by ambulance, and I can remember three things. The first was they couldn't tell how bad the injury was on the ultrasound, because there was so much blood. And then I remember my sister Melanie was there, and she was crying—she always cries. And finally I can remember saying to the doc as they were putting me out, 'Hey, make sure you save it.' It dawned on me that this was real life. I mean, I could lose it. When I came to the doc said he fixed it. He said it was like reverse peeling a banana, you know, peeling up instead of down."

Paul paused for a moment, thinking. "Certainly, when my wife says she has cramps, I respect what she's saying, there!"

SCRANTON: "What about now? How's life treating you?"

MOYER: "Well, I'm through playing football now. I don't know if I'd do it again, because now it's not short-term pain, that personal gratification of having doled out some punishment. Now I've got chronic pain, my neck and my back. I think several of my discs are crushed. I have pain every day. I encourage my son in every other sport but football. In America, your life expectancy is maybe 70, but I believe mine's been shortened because of the physical pounding."

SCRANTON: "Any words of wisdom for NFL players about getting ready for life after football?"

MOYER: "Build relationships. That is the biggest thing. Build relationships with the media, with people in the community, in business and so forth. Because you're going to need them at some point. What happens is that most players are sheltered. They think that they don't need to build relationships: they're making money, everybody wants them, blah, blah, blah. They are just so naïve and sheltered. Players should get into business from the start, even if they're working for free. Because some day they are going to have to go out there and actually work, even if they don't need the money. I mean, most of us guys are pretty competitive, and we've got to do at least something just to keep our minds going."

CURT WARNER   June 18, 1999, Seattle, Washington

It's 6:30 A.M., and Curt Warner and I are sitting in a quiet corner of the lobby of the downtown Seattle Westin Hotel. Curt has come up from his Vancouver, Washington, home to play in the Jacob Green Golf Classic. To date, the tournament has raised more than $600,000 for the Fred Hutchinson Cancer Center. Curt says he plays to an eight handicap, and he probably does. He plays golf the way he ran the ball: attack, attack, and attack! He looks lean and mean. If he had two percent body fat in the pros, he might have three percent now. Like me, he's lost a little hair since we first saw each other 16 years ago, but we don't talk about that. He runs a successful Chevrolet dealership in Vancouver, where he lives with his beautiful wife, Anna, and their three boys.

SCRANTON: "Where did you grow up, and where did you go to school?"

WARNER: "I was born in Pineville, West Virginia. I attended school at Pineville High, and I went on to Penn State, graduating in 1983."

SCRANTON: "As I recall, you had some success there, didn't you?" (Curt is modest and doesn't like to talk about himself. As long as I've known him, getting him to discuss his accomplishments has been a lot like pulling teeth.)

WARNER: "That's correct. I played at Penn State for Joe Paterno, and in 1983 we won the national championship. We beat Georgia 27–23 in the Sugar Bowl."

SCRANTON: "What's your best sports moment?"

WARNER: "I have had a lot of moments to remember, but one thing always comes to mind first—my first carry in the NFL. I broke through the line of scrimmage and went down the field for about 60 yards in Kansas City."

SCRANTON: "I remember that play, too. It was a pitch-out to the left. The safety had come up on the outside to force the play back in, but you cut inside and blew through his tackle. I believe it shocked Kansas City quite a bit."

WARNER: "It shocked me, too. It was the first time I touched the ball in the NFL, and bam! I was gone!"

SCRANTON: "What was it like coming out of college? What were the differences you saw between college and the pros?"

WARNER: "There were a number of things. First, there was a big difference in maturity as far as age, speed, and strength. In the pros, these were grown men, no red-shirt freshman running around out there. Second, the overall game was just much, much faster—extremely fast. And third, the pro game was more complex. There were a lot of different variations, a lot of different formations, defenses, and so forth. It was a big adjustment for me."

SCRANTON: "You once mentioned to me that it took you a while to get into the momentum of a game. How so?"

WARNER: "The longer I kept chipping away at the line, the more I was able to see the flow, and pick things up and run, and not have to think about it. As a running back, you know you're a wanted man. And when you get the football, you naturally think about that during the first part of the game. But as the game goes on, you kind of develop a sense of how the flow of the game is going, where the defensive schemes are, and as you get tired, the defense is also getting tired, and you start seeing more seams. It seemed to me that I used to get a little stronger as the game progressed, because I wasn't thinking anymore, I was just playing. In the beginning, I would get upset about getting hit, but finally, I didn't care whether I got hit. I just reacted."

SCRANTON: "Would you try to set up the defense?"

WARNER: "Well, yeah, to a certain degree. But a lot of it was instinct. I never really thought about the moves I made. I was just basically trying to get out of their way, and if a particular move worked, great. I might try something different the next time, but I didn't really have a preconceived notion of which way I wanted to go. The basic intention of a running back like me was to let my instincts take over. I didn't have that 230 or 240 pounds on my frame, so I couldn't just bowl someone over. It didn't take much, in my opinion, to run the football. I just had to be able to make my mind and body act in sync. Sometimes you can think about cutting right or cutting left, but if the body won't let you do it because your momentum is wrong, then you might be a step off, and you're going to go down."

SCRANTON: "It's September in Seattle. We're playing the opener against Cleveland. You went to the right on a sweep and hurt your knee. What happened?"

WARNER: "It was just your basic pitch play. You know, I remember the previous play so much better. I've replayed it in my mind a thousand times. It was a sweep to the other side, and had I gotten to the end zone and done what I was supposed to do that time, the next play wouldn't have been necessary. We wouldn't have had to come back to run the other sweep to the right. Well, we did run it, and I planned to go upfield like I'd done all through college and the pros a thousand times, and for whatever reason, the body was going one way, and the foot was going the other. I do remember the excruciating pain. My body and leg were going in opposite directions, and naturally, something had to give and I went down." (*I can still see the play. The O-line pulls to the right, Davey pitches the ball to Curt, and there's a lot of blocking and cutting as the play strings out sideways. Curt sees a seam and plants his right foot to cut into it. Suddenly his leg shudders, funny like, he kicks out in pain, and then he goes down like a sack of flour. Jimmy and I were running out onto the field before he hit the ground. Jimmy caught my eye, and we both knew even before we reached Curt, what had happened.*)

SCRANTON: "You had a hard time accepting what had happened at first. One of the things we talked about was the partnership between you, me, and Jimmy. But there was someone else in that partnership, too, wasn't there?"

WARNER: "Oh, without a doubt, Doc, it was my faith in the Lord Jesus Christ. And without that faith, and believing that if it was His will I would be able to play again, I don't think psychologically that I would have been able to get over the trauma of the whole thing. Basically, I had had no major physical injuries, and now, all of a sudden, here's a potential, career-ending injury. Thank God you didn't tell me at the time that it could be career ending. In fact, no one ever talked about it, and for the entire team, it was just a matter of my getting back in there and doing the rehab." (*During Curt's two days in the hospital, he became profoundly depressed. On the second day, Mike McCormack called me. "What's wrong? Why is he in so much pain, using narcotics all the time?" I took this call in my office. Suddenly a dark nightmare dawned on me, perhaps Curt's pain was a complication of a compartment syndrome! If he had had such a complication, it was already too late—two days post-operative and his leg muscles would be dead. I would have to leave town and abandon my practice because Curt would lose his leg. Later, my nurse told me that while I was talking to Mike, I turned chalk white, and beads of sweat stood out on my forehead. I put down the phone and told her to tell my patients that I needed to check on another patient at the hospital. I raced out of our office and ran the four blocks to the hospital. After charging up five flights of stairs to the orthopedic ward, I grabbed a pair of bandage scissors from the first nurse I saw. Puffing and panting, I must have seemed like a madman to Curt as I cut the dressing off his leg. The leg was normal. That's when I sat down on the bed, and we had our little chat about all the partners who were going to be involved in getting him better, starting right then.*)

SCRANTON: "What was it like, rehabbing with Jimmy?"

WARNER: (*C.W. grimaces, then grins.*) "Painful, very painful. Here's how it went with Jimmy. I was pretty much down there rehabbing seven to eight hours every day. I would go in in the morning to get the treatment, to get the 'stim' and crank the knee out a little bit. Jimmy's favorite instructions as he turned up the stim were, 'Tell me when it hurts.' And then he'd juice that thing until I'd almost come off the table! And I'd say, 'Jimmy, you *knew* that was going to hurt!' He'd laugh and turn it back down, and then we'd get on with therapy. It was pretty much an everyday ritual. I was going pretty hard, because I intended to get back out there and play again. But what would happen was, I would go for about three months, and then I would just burn out. Jimmy and I would get into a big fight and I'd leave for about three or four days. After about the third burnout, I could sense when it was going to happen. So I'd say, 'Jimmy, you know I've got to go home.' The first couple of times I had gotten mad and exploded in anger. 'I'm not going to do this anymore, and I'm just going to go home.' But after a while I'd come back mentally refreshed, and we'd get back at it again."

SCRANTON: "What was your best moment coming back?"

WARNER: "One of the first was in a game when my knee brace broke. I took a hit, and it broke. But I got back up and thought, 'Hey, my knee's okay.' I just got rid of it after that. I'd finally gotten over the psychological damage. You know, everybody treats the physical damage from an injury, but there's some psychological damage, too. You can't help remembering vividly what happened, and what you were capable of doing before the injury. So it does take some time. But when that brace finally broke, I knew I was okay.

"I was in the NFL for eight years. I had a number of good years after the injury. I was All-Pro in my rookie year and All-Pro two more years after my injury. As a matter of fact, in 1986, I had a fabulous year."

SCRANTON: "What advice do you have for the players who are in the league now?"

WARNER: "Make plans way ahead of the time you think you're going to retire. Naturally, you're thinking you'll never get hurt, and you're never going to retire—that's our mentality. But you *will* stop playing, and you *will* retire. So take the money, invest it, and make sure you are ready to make that transition. Somewhere along the line, somebody—the NFL, management, whoever—needs to introduce the players to corporate America and help them establish relationships. The NFL is pretty much based on now, and they don't think much about the future."

SCRANTON: "Do you think the player's association or the league could do a better job in preparing players for life after the NFL?"

WARNER: "I think both, because they each definitely have enough resources and funding. Someone has to shake reality into these players and say, 'Look, there's a lot of things out there.' They come and talk to us about drugs and NFL policy and so forth, but they never talk about, 'Hey, there *is* a life after, too, guys. Here are some things we can do for you, some programs we could get you involved in.' So somebody needs to help players find out what they could do and help them in the transition to get out there and do it."

EIGHT

Odds and Ends: The Supplementary Draft, Brian Bosworth, Women Reporters in the Locker Room, and the Hall of Fame

The Supplementary Draft

The NFL had always observed the sanctity of the undergraduate collegiate ranks, refusing to draft players until they had put in their four years and either graduated or been declared ineligible for further play. The NCAA and Divisions I through III had proven to be a great farm system for the NFL. Unlike the NBA or Major League Baseball, the NFL had demonstrated an appreciation for the way colleges winnowed out the cannon fodder and produced a valuable product for free. This non-tampering principle was respected for decades until finally a player and his agent sued the NFL, charging restraint of trade and collusion in blocking that player from his right to earn a living in the NFL. After all the lawyers got done talking about it, the NFL had to say, "Why not?" The floodgates opened. About 20 immature but talented juniors believed the wooing agents who told them they were actually good enough to grab some money and star in the NFL. It was sort of like the serpent telling Eve, "Go ahead, take a bite of the apple." The juniors declared themselves eligible. By signing with an agent, each gave up his right to a final year of NCAA eligibility. By the time the legal issues had been resolved, the regular draft was already under way. This led to the supplementary draft.

Initially, doctors and scouts were flown to Dallas to examine the juniors who'd turned out. None of these potential draft choices received the thorough exam they would have gotten at Indianapolis combines. There was a lot of agent hype. In the regular draft, the worst teams chose first, in order of their record—worst to best. In the supplementary draft, however, the order of choice was determined by lottery. If a team won the lottery and chose first and drafted a player, it gave up next year's first-round choice. If the team didn't want to lose next year's pick, it could pass and gamble that the player it wanted would be there in the second round. If the team took him then, it lost next year's second-round pick. The draft went for only five rounds. In the beginning, only a few players turned out for the supplementary draft. Eventually, the number stabilized at around 20 juniors.

In 1990, Emmitt Smith turned out early at the end of his junior year at the University of Florida. Jimmy Johnson had left the University of Miami to become head coach of the Dallas Cowboys. The Cowboys drew a high position in the lottery and immediately drafted Emmitt. As a result, they lost the following year's number-one draft choice. The Cowboys solved that problem by trading veteran running back Herschel Walker to the Minnesota Vikings, who in return relinquished almost all of their picks in the next draft. Smith went on to become one of the greatest rushers in NFL history.

Emmitt's story was unusual, though. In the early years, almost half of the juniors who turned out for the draft were not chosen. Since they had signed contracts with agents (for a few snazzy gold chains and a lot of promises), they forfeited their NCAA eligibility. They sued to get it back. They lost. Having bitten into the serpent's apple of greed, they were banned from the garden. Nowadays agents are very careful whom they advise to turn out for the draft. A player seeks a variety of expert opinions before risking his eligibility. But in the beginning, with the hype and the lure of big money, things got crazy. Naturally, the press didn't dwell on the losers. They showered attention on the high-profile winners who got big money. More juniors turned out early for the second supplementary draft. Their immaturity was immediately evident. They showed up at the tryouts with a cadre of handlers and agents loaded with press clippings, selected game films, and hype. Two quarterbacks from the PAC 10 turned out, got picked, and then their careers fell apart. They weren't ready for the pressure. I remember one year all the scouts were eagerly lined up with their stopwatches for the 40-yard dash. At the start line was the much-heralded Junior Seau strutting, puffing, and psyching himself up for the dash. Suddenly, without a word to anyone, he vanished from the field. No forty. The Chargers gambled anyway and took him in the first round. The Southern Cal Trojans were just an hour's drive up I–5. San Diego knew Junior's potential.

Brian Bosworth

Brian Bosworth, an early success story in the supplementary draft, was probably the most notorious and arguably one of the best linebackers ever to come from the University of Oklahoma. In his junior year, Oklahoma opened on the road against UCLA. UCLA was ranked number one in the nation—number one, that is, until they ran into The Boz. In that game, Bosworth single-handedly destroyed the UCLA offense. Anytime UCLA had the ball, from any formation, you could count on seeing Brian's form rocketing across the line through, over, or around the blockers, and knocking down the runner. This style of tackling would later come back to haunt him. He had supreme confidence in himself, and he finished the year with the Dick Butkus Award as the nation's best linebacker.

According to the NCAA, he had also tested positive for anabolic steroids. Brian's positive test and a stormy relationship with Coach Barry Switzer spilled into the news. Ultimately, Switzer held a press conference in which he announced that Brian would not be welcomed back in a Sooner uniform his senior year. So Brian decided to turn pro. His agent, Gary Wichard, announced that Brian would be eligible for the supplementary draft.

After not participating in the first two supplementary drafts, the Seattle Seahawks drew the first pick in the lottery in 1987. They promptly drafted Brian Bosworth. Mike McCormack excitedly ran down the halls at Seahawks headquarters crying, "We got him! We got him!" Chuck Knox was less than thrilled. He already had All-Pro Fred Young at Brian's position, and he was not happy about the potential for disruption of team chemistry, not to mention Brian's salary demands.

In hindsight, Chuck was right. Brian and his agent decided to hold out and demanded that the Seahawks trade Brian's rights to a big-market team like the Raiders, Giants, or Jets. The Seahawk management was patient and firm. There would be no trade. Numerous teams came sniffing. Would we consider one first-round draft choice for Brian? No. How about a first-round pick and a player? No. How about a first-round pick and a second-round pick? No. How about two first-round picks? No. The NFL scouts believed Brian had the potential to be one of the most dominating defensive players in league history. It became a matter of principle for the Seahawk owners that they draft a deal to land the day's biggest name in sports. Don't dis' Seattle and the Pacific Northwest!

Brian continued his holdout, as did Mike McCormack. Brian complained in the press; Mike had no comment other than to say that the Seahawks did not negotiate contracts in the press. Training camp started at the new Kirkland headquarters, and still no Brian. Quietly, Mike McCormack waited out Brian and Gary Wichard with the confidence of a man who knows he's got a prime fish hooked on a strong leader with the drag set just right. The standoff continued for over a month. Mike was always polite, always ready to talk, and always declined trade offers. Exhibition games came and went. Practices continued.

Finally McCormack wore them down. Brian signed, and the city went crazy. A shiny black limo met Brian and Gary Wichard at the SeaTac Airport gate. He was whisked right off the tarmac and out of the reach of hundreds of curious fans. He had already missed three quarters of summer training camp, and therefore the Seahawks thought that even that afternoon's practice was important. I got a call from McCormack while I was in the Providence Hospital operating room. The Boz couldn't step onto the field without a physical; the whole contract was dependent on his passing that exam. Mike needed me there yesterday. I was in Seattle, in the operating room, and rush-hour traffic clogged the floating bridges to Kirkland. Maybe in an hour, I told him, maybe an hour and a half. Mike went crazy. He called back. "Finish your case, and then go to Harborview Hospital and wait at the heliport." I did. Paul Brindle from the KIRO News got permission from the FAA to pick me up and fly me to an empty schoolyard near Seahawk headquarters. News of my helicopter ride went out on the traffic radio, and fans cheered at the schoolyard as I jumped in the waiting van to go to headquarters.

When I got there, no Brian! His agent had diverted the limo to Children's Hospital where Brian posed for pictures with some sick and injured children. The PR message was supposed to be that Brian cared so much about children that he'd rather see them than sign a deal for millions. Let the Seahawks wait.

What kind of guy was Brian Bosworth? Actually, he was an extremely pleasant, articulate team player. He apologized for being late, mumbling with a wry smile about getting "some agent stuff" out of the way. He had a totally normal physical. He was benching over 300 pounds. He had never been injured, never been operated upon, and had never missed a practice.

Just like that. I shook his hand at the end of the physical as I always did. "Good luck, and welcome to Seattle."

True to Chuck Knox's prediction, linebacker Fred Young immediately missed a practice because he was unhappy. The team chemistry was altered. The defensive schemes that Chuck and Tom Catlin had instituted now needed tinkering. Tom spent hours and hours during and after practice, trying to teach Brian the complicated schemes.

Although Brian professed that he wanted to be a team player and become part of the Seahawks, his alter ego, "The Boz," had other plans. The Boz was Brian's public personae, carefully cultivated by Brian and Gary Wichard. It was the alter ego who was brash, audacious, outrageous, and loud, who bragged about spitting a loogie in the face of a downed opponent.

In the locker room after every game, Chuck never failed to mention that the players should *keep their mouths shut!* There was to be no gloating, no boasting, nothing to fuel the fires of the enemy press for the following week's game. After one unremarkable game, The Boz announced to the press that it was his intention to personally seek out and, if he could, hurt Denver's quarterback, John Elway, during our road trip to Denver the following week. A nuclear bomb might as well have gone off. To Denver, Elway was a sacred treasure—mother's milk and the American flag rolled into one. Thousands of outraged fans crowded the talk-show airways. They demanded that the referees watch The Boz, eject The Boz, or suspend The Boz if he so much as looked cross-eyed at Elway. A new T-shirt appeared. It was white with a "Ban The Boz" logo on the front. The T-shirt sold out in a matter of days, and at Mile High Stadium that weekend, Bronco orange was replaced with these white T-shirts—all sold by Brian Bosworth and his agent!

Elway seemed to have been unnerved. His timing was off during the game. Several times he scampered out of the pocket early or rushed his passes. Once he rolled to his left and got sacked by our safety with The Boz not far behind. He yelled something at Brian, and Brian took off his helmet to show the nation the Seahawk colors dyed into his Mohawk. Chuck Knox was not amused.

The Seahawks ground through the rest of the season without a trip to the playoffs. Fred Young was eventually traded to the Indianapolis Colts for two first-round picks, and Brian became assimilated into the Seahawks. He worked hard to be a team player, but his outrageous personae ruined his private life. He was mobbed everywhere he went. He could not have a quiet meal in a restaurant. He could not shop. He could not go to any public event without hoards of autograph seekers pestering him. However, he could, with the help of Rick Kelly, write a book—*Brian Bosworth: Confessions of a Modern Anti-Hero.* It was released just before the next season and included a widely publicized remark about "old horse-face," Denver's overrated quarterback, John Elway. The Denver fans, wise to the "Ban The Boz" trickery, didn't buy T-shirts this time. On the Denver sports talk shows, a caller suggested that The Boz's book was so obscene and stupid that they should have a Bronco pep rally where everyone would bring a copy of the book to burn it. This pep rally was a huge success, with thousands of fans purchasing books to burn them. The caller I believe was Gary Wichart.

It wasn't long before Brian's tackling technique began to catch up with him. In college, his 244 pounds was usually enough to knock a running back down. In the pros, however, unless you wrapped up the running back, the technique didn't cut it. Probably Brian's most famous on-the-field exploit is the tackle that never was. Brian was bulldozed into the end zone on ABC's *Monday Night Football* by the Raiders' Bo Jackson. To me it seemed that Brian had disproportionately small hands and arms for his frame. Knocking people down with a spearing shoulder had been his trademark. In a home game against the Washington Redskins, he attempted an arm tackle. The running back ran right through his outstretched arm, severely wrenching his shoulder. We were surprised when our X rays showed severe arthritis in the shoulder joint. The arthritic spurs were debrided arthroscopically in the off-season, and Brian went through extensive rehabilitation. The cause of the arthritic damage was a mystery. During the next season, out of the blue, the opposite shoulder suffered the same fate.

Severe arthritis in both shoulders ended Brian's career in the NFL. Brian was a twenty-five-year-old with the shoulders of a sixty-year-old. He flunked my physical, and his Lloyd's of London insurance contract should have kicked in. However, they claimed fraud and refused to pay, maintaining that Brian had the disease arthritis, not a work-related injury. Brian sued Lloyd's of London, and so did the Seahawks. If a loophole existed in the insurance policy, the Seahawks were next on the hook, and the money would count against the cap. In Judge Dyer's federal court, with Jimmy and me testifying for Brian, Lloyd's of London was found in breach of contract and was ordered to pay Brian's guaranteed salary *plus interest*. In lawyerly fashion, Lloyd's threatened to drag things out with a prolonged appeal unless Brian agreed to the salary only—forget the interest. Brian ultimately went on to Hollywood to make movies, the Seahawks went back to team football, and The Boz vanished.

Women Reporters in the Locker Room

Until recently, the role of women in professional football had been pretty clearly defined. They were peripheral. A "good" coach's wife was supposed to be quiet, supportive, and loyal, a background figure mostly involved in raising the family or participating in charity fund-raisers. The only other women in football were the cheerleaders. They were supposed to be sexy but wholesome (you can look, but don't touch), active in team promotions and charities. Professional team cheerleaders who appeared in *Playboy* or *Penthouse* were either fired on the spot or just didn't make the team the next year.

The NFL, always seeking to expand its market, recognized that football was perceived almost exclusively as a man's game. The clichéd "football widows"—wives abandoned on weekends by husbands glued to the television screen—represented a largely untapped market. How about a female reporter, someone to add color commentary? Perhaps if women viewers identified with a female football reporter, more women would watch the games, boosting Nielsen ratings and advertising revenue! Since no one was opposed to more money the NFL figured, why not?

The first professional football game to feature a female sideline reporter pitted the Seahawks against the Chiefs. Katie Couric was chosen to be the groundbreaking announcer. I believe she later indicated that she was quite nervous being the first woman on the field of battle in this otherwise male domain. She interviewed each coach for 30 seconds at halftime. I never did hear what Chuck Knox thought. I never did see her, nor did I see a clip of her interviews. It was the middle of winter on a cold night in Kansas City, we were taking our usual drubbing at the hands of the Chiefs, and I had many injuries to attend.

It was really a non-event. Katie did not pave the way for a future female anchor. In the decade since, there has never been a female commentator in the booth doing play-by-play with the likes of John Madden, Pat Summerall, and Al Michaels. To date, female commentators have only made sideline reports or asked carefully rehearsed inane questions like, "Coach, can your O-line adjust at halftime to stop those blitzing defensive ends who sacked your quarterback six times in the first half?" The fact is, very few women have played the game above the high-school level, except for a rare curiosity place kicker in college. Football is a man's sport. Men are from Mars and women are from Venus, and they can't comment on football as knowledgeably as men because they do not understand male camaraderie or the nuances of the trenches.

Though Katie Couric's stint in the NFL didn't lead to female commentators in the booth, it did raise a difficult question. If female reporters could cover the sidelines, why couldn't they also cover the locker rooms? Was it really fair to deny them access when all the male reporters got to go right in? It was discrimination, legally speaking. Certain female reporters claimed that they had as much a right to an on-the-spot interview as did any male reporter. To deny them immediate access was to prevent them from doing their job. Linda Cohn of ESPN was still a fledgling minor sports anchor in Seattle at that time. She correctly pointed out that there was no substitute for the immediate, spontaneous response of an excited athlete after a game. To wait a half-hour or an hour was to lose that moment. Translation: If we can get to the athletes early, they'll say things that are emotionally charged, stupid, sensational, controversial, and reportable. A female reporter had as much right to that sound bite as a male.

Facing threats of discrimination lawsuits, the NFL caved. In 1990, female reporters were granted the same locker-room access as male reporters. But while the NFL acquiesced to the legal right of female reporters to enter a locker room, they did not respond to the players' right for privacy. To have a female reporter suddenly enter a male locker room filled with sweaty, exhausted men in various stages of nakedness heading for the showers *was* offensive. The players might be professional athletes, but they were still men, deserving the same dignified treatment that any woman would demand. When Lisa Olson of the *Boston Herald* entered the New England Patriots locker room, the men reacted with predictable hostility. She was harassed, humiliated, and left in tears. She later sued the Patriots. But was it really fair to those disrobing men to have a female walking around in their midst?

Sam Wyche of the Cincinnati Bengals reacted with outrage. He denied *all reporters* access to the Bengals' locker room until the players were dressed. The league fined him $10,000. Finally the league began providing "privacy towels" to protect the players' privacy. Before reporters were allowed into the locker room, a brief delay gave players time to get out of their uniforms and into their covering towels before granting interviews. This policy ended the battle of the politically correct equal-rights opportunists. But one might wonder if there is still a double standard. Are male reporters given equal access to the women's locker room in the WNBA?

These events involved legal issues of equal access and discrimination, but they also crossed into matters of human dignity, modesty, and the right to privacy. No individual has the right to view another naked without that individual's consent. As a physician and surgeon, I have always seen my patients in private examination rooms. Male or female patients are seen in appropriate examining gowns that respect their modesty and right to privacy. While the NFL bowed to the letter of the law on the issue of discrimination and equal access, the league might have better served its players by first inquiring about their desires regarding modesty and privacy. The league could have had an appropriate policy in place first *before* a reporter got humiliated, before the outrage of players and coaches spilled into the headlines. The NFL lawyers might have asked a doctor.

The Hall of Fame

The Hall of Fame is a must-see for anyone devoted to football. Founded on September 17, 1920, in an old car dealership, the Hall of Fame is located in Canton, Ohio, on George Halas Drive. Today, the remodeled Hall is housed in a circular museum wrapped around a football-like central tower. My first trip to Canton was in 1984 when the Seahawks opened the season in an exhibition game against the Tampa Bay Buccaneers at the Hall of Fame Game. Our own general manager, Mike McCormack, was inducted into the Hall of Fame that year. It was a special feeling watching him ride for a victory lap around the field in a convertible, the crowd cheering him all the way. As a young boy, I'd watched Mike leading Jim Brown into the end zone, now Mike joined him in the Hall. Mike's bronze bust is on display along with video clips of some of the great plays.

The museum is absolutely first class, taking you back past even the roots of the NFL to the early twenties, to the Akron Pros, the Canton Bulldogs, and to Jim Thorpe of the American Professional Football Association. You'll see their uniforms, clips of their exciting plays, and witness the formation of the NFL by George Halas in 1922. You'll watch old film of the great Red Grange shedding blockers and juking D backs, and you'll have the opportunity to see some of the great playoff games of the age. We went back to the Hall of Fame in 1997 just to see Steve Largent's bronze bust. We were in Ohio, playing the Cincinnati Bengals, and I wanted one last look. Jimmy, Hal Kuhlgren, and I drove up on a foggy Saturday night. The security guards had been alerted, and they graciously let us in. In retrospect, I think I'd still like to see the Hall one more time but spend a whole day there or more.

NINE

The Good, the Bad, and the Ugly:
The League Office, Owners, Coaches, and Agents

During my tenure as a team physician, the Seahawks and the league as a whole experienced considerable change. The relationship between the league commissioner, the owners, the players, the NFL Players Association, and the agents is always evolving. Money, of course, is the primary driving force behind the changes in these relationships. There are billions and billions of dollars to be made from television contracts, stadium revenue, advertising, product endorsements, depreciation, and tax breaks. The balancing forces are the same in the NFL as in any other industry: fear and greed. Unfettered, the owners, players, and agents would behave like a bunch of wild cats thrown into a bag. However, through the auspices of the NFL Commissioner's Office and the NFL Players Agreement, they all link arms, march in step, and pick up their fair shares of the loot. This chapter represents my medical perspective on the league as a whole, opinions no doubt different from those of, say, Gene Upshaw of the players union or Al Davis.

The League Office
In their wisdom, the owners recognized that they needed to save themselves from themselves. Imagine a whole bunch of millionaires in the same room. Some are self-made, hard-driving tycoons, canny, conniving, ruthless, and boorish men who frequently have made their money by clawing and scraping through life, selling cars, dealing real estate or commodities, leveraging and litigating. Still others have been shrewd in businesses such as oil, clothing stores, shipping, and information services. The lucky ones woke up in a bassinet only to hear a man's voice say, "Some day, little guy, this will all be yours."

Diverse as the owners are, they recognized that a house divided against itself cannot stand. Therefore they agreed to give up some degree of power, believing in the end that they would benefit (i.e., make even more money). Pete Rozelle, the first strong NFL commissioner, proved them correct. He oversaw the merger of the AFL and NFL into today's NFL. He also got tough with the television networks, playing one against the other to negotiate a blockbuster contract giving the NFL owners more money than they had ever imagined. NFL Properties took shape, and the NFL began endorsing products. *Monday Night Football* became a religion.

We NFL doctors had little exposure to Pete Rozelle, but in my experience, he was a very gracious man. I met him in the Kingdome training room before an ABC *Monday Night Football* game. He had a minor medical problem, and our internist, Jim Trombold, and I were happy to offer assistance. In the course of treating I kidded him about his fastidious dress and Palm Beach tan. He shrugged and smiled. When one represented the league and was in the public eye at all times, he said, a meticulous attention to appearance was the rule. A week later, I opened an envelope from 410 Park Avenue, New York City. It contained a brief, handwritten note thanking us for our kind efforts on his behalf. He was, in fact, recovering nicely. To me, this demonstration of thoughtfulness, of common courtesy, revealed him to be a very gracious man. Pete Rozelle is now enshrined in the Football Hall of Fame.

When Rozelle retired, a new commissioner had to be chosen. With the evolving complexity of contracts, drug testing, labor issues, and the plethora of lawsuits filed by agents, municipalities, and various owners against the league, it was obvious that the NFL needed a man with a legal background. It would have been fun to be a fly on the wall during this election. In the end, the owners chose Paul Tagliabue. By all accounts, he appears to be a man who understands the legal complexities of running the NFL's multibillion-dollar corporation. Every day his office tackles problems such as medical malpractice, television contracts, athletic equipment contracts, player union contracts, quarreling litigious owners, and medical care for teams in a foreign country during an exhibition game. For now, Paul Tagliabue seems to have a benevolent despot's magic touch.

When Tagliabue took the job, the NFL Physicians Society decided to become proactive. In the past, the league had issued mandates on medical equipment, sideline support, and so forth, without any real input from team physicians. At the time, Dr. Mike Dillingham of the 49ers was president, Dr. Lon Castle of the Cleveland Browns was vice president, and I was next in line. We wrote Commissioner Tagliabue a letter and invited him to meet with us at the February Indianapolis combines. Would he consider addressing our society? He accepted, and we had a cordial meeting for about an hour in a suite at the Westin Hotel across from the Hoosier Dome. The commissioner confessed that, frankly, he'd never even heard of us. His previous NFL experience had been with a club whose team physicians weren't heavily involved in our organization.

As a result of that meeting, the NFL Physicians Society formed a very good relationship with the commissioner's office. We became what we should have been all along, a medical-knowledge resource for the commissioner's staff at 410 Park Avenue. Tagliabue ultimately wound up forming the NFL Safety Committee, and the NFL Physicians Society president was always asked to be present at the meetings. Commissioner Tagliabue recognized the important role of the sideline team physicians. He also recognized that the league needed to set standards for the delivery of care. The NFL Players Association also participated in setting standards, requiring that a board-certified orthopedic surgeon be available to the players of every club, as well as an NATA-certified trainer. Regulations were established regarding heat and humidity limits during practice and low game temperatures in the winter. We were consulted regarding shoe safety and some of the multimillion-dollar contracts that the league had signed for their officially endorsed shoes. Were these shoes unsafe? There was discussion about whether the league could be held liable for promoting certain shoes that might make players be predisposed to injury. What did we think about providing Gatorade on the sidelines? Hence the NFL physicians and the league developed a closer relationship. We also tried to develop a relationship with the players association, but they declined the invitation to address our society. To the best of my knowledge, no real meaningful contacts have been made with Gene Upshaw.

During my years in the NFL, I couldn't really say whether injuries were becoming more frequent. The injuries certainly began to attract more negative publicity, though. Football players had become household names. O.J. leapt over chairs in the airport, Steve Largent appeared on a cereal box, and on television Dan Marino showed you what gloves to buy at Christmas. Now these same stars were being carted off the field, writhing in agony, while the plays on which they were injured were shown repeatedly from multiple angles and in slow motion. We got to see the Redskins' Joe Theisman grotesquely break his leg. During the Super Bowl, we watched Tim Krumrie of the Bengals break his leg, too. Atlanta quarterback Chris Miller ended up unconscious on the turf again and again and again.

The NFL's image began to suffer as this "epidemic" of injuries was chronicled in *Sports Illustrated* and elsewhere in the media. The press speculated that the league's greedy, filthy-rich owners were insensitive to the pain and devastating injuries among their golden stars. The media hyped the idea that the owners viewed the players as nothing more than commodities—depreciated meat. Suit up the next one! To combat this publicity, Tagliabue convened the NFL Safety Committee. The committee was comprised of independent researchers, internists, a referee representative (Jerry Seamans), Jan van Duser from the league office, and a member of our society. The committee's charge was to address the pressing issues of player safety.

During my two years on the committee, four specific tasks were accomplished. We investigated the relationship between the playing surface (natural and artificial) and injuries. The hype surrounding hyperbaric oxygen led us to investigate whether this kind of treatment was beneficial. We set up a study protocol to learn more about the incidence, presentation, and management of concussions and head injuries. And finally, we made recommendations on which research projects were worthy of NFL Charities funding.

Our task was to try to apply science to safety problems. We needed to see the whole picture, not get wrapped up in media hype surrounding a single high-profile player's injury. For example, when the Steelers' All-Pro Rod Woodson blew out the anterior cruciate ligament in his knee, the media immediately began screaming about how dangerous Astroturf was. On TV, the media played and replayed the image of Rod getting hurt, pointing out that no one had even touched him. Commentators speculated that most tragic injuries could have been prevented if only the money-grubbing owners had been willing to pay for natural grass. Agents and players were quoted saying that they would refuse to play for any team that didn't have a natural grass field.

The problem was, no one really knew the injury rate on grass versus turf. So we decided to find out. Our good friend John Powell was also on the NFL

Safety Committee. John ran the NAIRS (National Athletic Injury Reporting System) program using data on thousands of injuries from more than a decade of collegiate and professional sports. In his initial review, Astroturf was linked to a higher injury rate. However, this data included non-catastrophic injuries such as mat burns, concussions, knee pain, and shin splints (tendonitis). We wanted to look more closely at the relationship between turf and serious, career-threatening injuries.

We formed a study group—funded by NFL Charities and approved by the Safety Committee—to examine the incidence of noncontact knee blowouts on Astroturf versus natural grass. A noncontact injury is one that doesn't involve contact with other players. For example, when an athlete is bulldozed by an opponent and suffers a broken leg, that's a contact injury. When an athlete runs down the field and pulls a hamstring—without anyone touching him—that's a noncontact injury. Catastrophic knee injury can occur when a football player is sprinting down the field and he zigs, but his knee zags.

In the course of this study, we examined 75 NFL players who had suffered noncontact knee blowouts. We recorded the condition of the field (wet or dry), the type of surface (natural or artificial), and the type of shoe, with or without a tape job or "spat." To our amazement, we found it was far more dangerous to run and cut on a natural grass field wearing traditional football cleats than it was to play on an artificial surface. There were three times as many knee blowouts on natural grass as on artificial turf. In other words, if a player's cleats got caught in the sod for just an instant, the torque on the leg could blow out the knee. In the lab, we measured this force to be as high as 12 times body weight! Let's put this into football perspective: If a 200-pound running back squirts through the gap in the line and jukes a linebacker in the secondary and is unfortunate enough to catch his cleats on the turf, he can generate 2,400 pounds/inch/second^2 of torque—more than ample force to shred his knee's anterior cruciate ligament.

Based on our findings, we felt the risks of noncontact injuries could be minimized with proper footwear. On natural grass with good footing, we recommended to the league that players use shorter cleats. On astroturf, we believed that a flatter shoe surface such as that on a court shoe (like those used in basketball) would be safer. If a player wanted to use a multi-studded turf shoe, he could have the trainer put a taped spat over the ball of the sole to minimize the risk that the shoe would momentarily bond to the turf. The long-term effects of these recommendations won t be known for several years, but if our recommendations helped prevent just one knee blowout, to me it will have been worth it.

The next issue the NFL Safety Committee tackled was hyperbaric oxygen, a treatment that gained media attention after the Vancouver Canucks enjoyed great success in the Stanley Cup playoffs. The Canucks had suffered a rash of player injuries during the season. These players were treated by conventional means, but they also received hyperbaric oxygen treatments in a decompression chamber. This unconventional treatment was trumpeted as a cure-all. The manufacturer claimed it accelerated healing. Soon teams in the NBA, the NFL, and Major League Baseball all wanted to know, What the heck was hyperbaric oxygen? Should they be running out to spend millions of dollars for hyperbaric chambers?

The NFL Safety Committee put hyperbaric oxygen on its agenda for our May 1995 meeting in Cleveland. We brought in experts in pulmonary physiology and wound healing to discuss their findings with us. What we learned represented a confusing array of true science and a nightmare of risks and medicolegal exposure. On the plus side, we found some basic science studies that showed that 100% oxygen treatments at twice atmospheric pressure enhanced tissue repair. In other words, if you crushed the muscles of a bunch of rabbits and one half of the rabbits got the oxygen while the other half didn t, the oxygen group experienced better healing. So should we all jump on this bandwagon and start sucking oxygen?

Unfortunately, there were too many risks. First, as any scuba diver knows, being under pressure at two atmospheres entails significant cardiac and pulmonary risks. There is also an estimated one-in-a-thousand risk of seizure during decompression. You might think, One in a thousand that s not all that bad. Not all that bad, huh? How d you like to be the one having the seizure? Or look at it from the perspective of a doctor who must watch his patient have a seizure in a decompression chamber while he s helpless on the outside.

Claustrophobia is an issue, too. Imagine the following scenario: Mr. Macho football player, refusing to show any fear, swaggers up and climbs into the chamber for his sprained-ankle treatment. The chamber is sealed, and as he cycles down to two atmospheres of oxygenated pressure, his bravado crumbles. A full-blown panic attack ensues. Best-case scenario: he doesn't further injure himself before the chamber can cycle back. Worse case? You go figure.

Finally, exactly who is going to administer these treatments? And who is going to decide which injuries warrant treatment and which do not? In the state of Washington, it's not legal for a trainer to administer any treatment except under the direction of a doctor. How'd you like to be a player in a chamber having a seizure, with no skilled nurse or doctor available? Or how'd you like to be a doctor with an office full of sick and injured patients waiting for you while you're sitting outside a decompression chamber as the trainer ushers in 20 players with turf burns, contusions, and sprains? In the end, the safety committee chose to identify the benefits and risks of hyperbaric oxygen treatment and to educate the teams and their players. Those players who wished to have hyperbaric treatment could get it, but on their own, not under the auspices of the NFL.

The final issue we looked at during my time with the NFL Safety Committee was concussion management. This problem is so complex, so scientific, that even though our study was initiated during my presidency on the committee in 1997, it's still ongoing. We used to think that concussions could be simply understood according to the Maron Classification: Grade I meant you were dazed, you got your bell rung. Grade II meant you were knocked unconscious, but only for a few seconds. Grade III meant you were unconscious for more than one minute. A player's return to a game was predicated on these classifications. A Grade I concussion was supposed to be benign. There were jokes about dazed players staggering around on the field. We hadn't yet learned that brain damage had no relationship to the grade of concussion.

The long-term, cumulative effects of concussions aren't yet fully understood. But then, we didn't know that one concussion put a player at higher risk of additional concussions. What happened when you were repeatedly knocked silly? Punch-drunk ex-boxers were the only popular frame of reference. Quarterback Chris Miller had so many concussions with the Atlanta Falcons and the St. Louis Rams that the doctors retired him medically. He was still in his prime. Years later he tried to come back, so he was studied by all kinds of experts using neurological tests, MRIs, and EEGs. He was cautiously declared fit, and he returned to play for the Denver Broncos. He took one wrong hit, and bang! He went back out. The same problem forced

Steve Young and Troy Aikman to retire. Quarterbacks are particularly vulnerable to concussions because they have to stand tall in the pocket, waiting to
unload the ball before they get hit. Remember that Astroturf is not much
more than a rug on cement—not gentle on the skull. Getting your brain
bruised and permanently damaged is serious business. But if I tried to discuss
all the factors associated with concussions, I'm afraid it would make *you*
unconscious! So I won't.

Each of the committee's sessions ended with the happier task of reviewing
the grant requests for NFL Charities. Over the years, the foundation has
granted millions of dollars to fund serious research. For example, NFL
Charities has supported the Nick Buonocoti Spinal Cord Paralysis Research
Institute. They've spent hundreds of thousands of dollars investigating helmet
design, shock absorption, and developing better ways to treat injuries to the
knee. They've supported projects to study and investigate better shoe design
with safer surface-interface characteristics. We reviewed each of the submitted
projects and made recommendations. Curiously, to the best of my knowledge,
the NFL Players Association does not appear to be involved in any way in
funding safety research.

The NFL's obsession with its image colors every aspect of the league's
relationship with the public, the players, team management—and even us
doctors. Consider the problem of gambling. More than a billion dollars were
bet via the Internet on the Super Bowl in 1999, a sum that doesn't include
wagers in Las Vegas, Atlantic City, or office pools, let alone your local corner
bookie. Even the remote suspicion of a shaved point or a thrown game could
jeopardize the NFL's image, so the league is vigilant in keeping up appearances
when it comes to gambling. Many years ago, my partner, Walter Krengel,
was finishing up an injury clinic for the Seahawks. He mentioned to the
coach that he had to hurry because he was going to be late for our office's
business meeting, which had been scheduled at a local restaurant. Several
days later, he got a call from the NFL league office's security division. The
restaurant he'd mentioned was on a list of establishments identified by the
NFL as "possible" sites of numbers operations. For *appearance's sake,* Dr.
Krengel was advised that, in the future, our meetings should be held elsewhere.

The league has also waged war against illegal drug trafficking and the
use of steroids, which threaten fair competition in the NFL. Anabolic steroids

can produce muscle-bound freaks who are disproportionately large for their frames. Further, most of these drugs were manufactured illegally in Mexican or South American pharmaceutical plants. These illegal factories produced steroids that had unknown purity, sterility, and concentrations. The illegal labs would counterfeit labels from trusted pharmaceutical companies such as Eli Lilly and Pfizer, so that users would believe that the drugs had come from a reputable manufacturer.

The health risks of these street steroids were largely unknown because nobody actually knew what chemicals the players were ingesting and in what concentrations. Hypogonadism, sterility, adrenal shutdown, cardiomyopathy, psychotic breakdowns, suicide, and even leukemia could *still* be ticking time bombs in those players who used these illegal drugs. Around the same time that steroid use mushroomed, the rise of crack cocaine posed a second—and even more deadly—risk to players. The league had to act.

The commissioner's office announced a program of random drug testing. Fortunately, all the by-products of anabolic steroids, narcotics, and even chronic alcohol abuse can be discovered in a urine sample. If your number was randomly drawn by a computer, you peed in a little bottle. The NFL Players Association called the policy an unconscionable invasion of privacy. I believe the association's outrage was all politics and posturing. Soon they agreed to the testing and it was written into their NFL Players Contract. For its part, the league offered a system of graduated penalties and help—the carrot and the stick. A first offense warranted a brief suspension and mandated counseling, rehabilitation, and an NFL lifetime of random urine sampling. Second offense was a one-year suspension, more counseling, and continued testing. Third strike? You're out! Let's call this system "zero tolerance with compassion." But it has worked. The system offers an interesting contrast to Major League Baseball or the NBA, where the drug programs have no real clout. Baseball players can come back again and again and again. In the NBA, it's almost like, "Uh, you aren't using any drugs, are you?"

"Gee, no."

"Great. I was kind of hoping you'd say that."

Owners

Many years ago, when the late Malcolm Forbes was the editor of *Forbes* magazine, an interviewer challenged him, claiming that his articles on corporations were one-sided. He chastised Malcolm for not interviewing workers and middle management. Why did Malcolm interview only CEOs? Malcolm counterattacked: if he looked the CEO in the eye, asked tough questions, saw his body language, and followed his thought processes as he responded to the questions, then Malcolm knew all he needed to know about that company. I believe Malcolm was right. Essentially, if you have a jerk at the top, it's reflected through the whole corporation. But I also believe you can look at the "little people" at the bottom of a corporation and learn a lot, too. You can see how the company is run by the way they're treated, and you can then extrapolate to determine what kind of management resides at the top.

Consider the Colts. In the early 1980s, the famous Mayflower moving-van episode occurred when the Colts ownership sneaked the team out of Baltimore in the wee hours of the morning. The owners knew they were abandoning their fans and the Colt heritage; but once they got to Indianapolis, the franchise immediately began to make a lot of money. The city had been desperate for some kind of identity apart from the Indy 500. The Hoosier Dome had been built with public money, and the city offered the Colts a sweet financial deal. The Colts drafted John Elway, but despite the prospect of great wealth, John mistrusted the team's management. He refused to report, threatened to sit out a year, and got himself traded. Jeff George got drafted, but after years of turmoil, he too demanded to get out. The Colts' doctor, Don Shelbourne, complained to me he was worried about getting sued because management would ignore his advice and cut an injured player. Eventually, Don was let go. Even a blind hog finds an acorn now and then, and after years of high draft picks, the Colts got lucky. The team's emotional momentum got them within one play of the Super Bowl, but management's response was to promptly fire the coach who got them there, Ted Marchibroda. They also figured out a way to make millions more, renaming the Hoosier Dome after the highest bidder, RCA. Then they hired and fired coach Lindy Infante. Finally, almost 20 years after the Mayflower move, they hired a classy general manager, Bill Polian, and a savvy head coach, Jim Mora, each of whom knew football. But how long will the team's success last before ownership interferes again? In this brief history, you can see the effect of ownership's character on the fortunes of a franchise.

I don't mean to single out one team for the character of its owners. To some extent, the league can't help breeding selfish arrogance. Everybody who owns a team is a gazillionaire, and they didn't get that way by being nice guys. The purpose of owning a team is to be able to walk around with an ostentatious diamond ring that announces to the world, "I'm the best." The game itself has no remorse. At the end of each season, there is only one Super Bowl winner—all the rest are "losers." The coaches understand this— win or you're gone. There is no loyalty except to winning. In the NFL, owners and coaches can treat employees in ways that would immediately provoke a successful lawsuit in any other business. They say that NFL stands for Not For Long, and graciousness is a word not generally found in the league's vocabulary.

This lack of graciousness and loyalty is epitomized in the treatment of head trainer George Anderson. After more than 30 years of loyal service, George had a run-in with his owner. He refused to speak at a press conference to denounce a former team physician who had written a negative book about the Raiders. George's wife was fighting cancer, and the book's author was her doctor. So George became a nonperson. Later, when his dear wife, Marcy, died, he told me that every team in the NFL sent flowers to the funeral. Every team except the Raiders.

One of my last acts as president of the NFL Physicians Society was to establish a new award to counteract this crass insensitivity. This award was to be given each year to an NFL trainer who, in the opinion of the Professional Football Athletic Trainers Society (PFATS) and the NFL Physicians Society, deserved recognition for his excellence and devotion to the care of his athletes. We decided to name this award the Cain-Fain NFL Physicians Society Award.

Tom Cain and Robert Fain Sr. were orthopedic surgeons who practiced in Houston. They were not partners, but they had been the founding orthopedic doctors for the Houston Oilers. They were collegial, and they devoted their professional careers to caring for their team, its coaches, management, and personnel. In their community, they were liked, and throughout the league, they were respected. As the decades went by, Robert Fain Sr. began to cut back his practice, and his son Bob Jr. assumed a larger role with the Oilers while still working with Tom Cain.

In 1993, two expansion teams were founded, the Carolina Panthers and Jacksonville Jaguars (they would not begin league play until 1995). The Jaguars needed capital, and they hit upon the innovative idea of having health plans bid on the right to take care of their athletes. In return, the winning plan could advertise that it was the provider of medical care for the Jaguars. Never mind that in medicine, advertising has always been regarded as unethical—if you're good, let your work speak for itself. Health South won the bid, and the Jaguars netted seven figures of additional revenue.

Sports Illustrated ran an article on the conflicts of interest faced by medical doctors who are hired to care for athletes by companies that bid on the right to advertise that care. This article highlighted the Boston Red Sox and the Jacksonville Jaguars. The Jaguars ignored the criticism. For their part, the Oilers' management seemed to smell money. "Who in Houston would like to pay for the right to advertise that they care for the Oilers?" A frenzied bidding took place between two corporations, Health South and Columbia Health. Tom Cain was dying of cancer, and Robert Fain Sr. had retired. Never mind. There was no farewell dinner or even a pat on the back. The Oilers notified Tom by fax that he needn't bother coming around anymore.

In 1994, I called Tom Cain to ask permission to use his name on this award. He broke down and cried when I told him the purpose of the award. The first Cain-Fain NFL Physicians Award went to George Anderson of the Los Angeles Raiders for unrecognized excellence and service. Tom Cain, a wonderful physician and a gentleman, died a week later. The Oilers escaped Houston to Tennessee, where they played the same bidding game again. This time, it was Columbia Health versus Baptist Hospital. Baptist Hospital's management was foolish enough to pony up $45,000,000 for the right to say that Baptist provided care for the Tennessee Titans. The deal led to such disgust among hospital staff and in the medical community that the repercussions have not yet subsided. Does any Titans player wonder why he is so strongly encouraged to get his operation at Baptist?

Year in and year out, some teams are always in the hunt come playoff time—San Francisco, Dallas, Denver, Buffalo, Green Bay. Given revenue sharing, the reverse order of the draft, and weaker schedules for weaker teams, it's hard for a team to repeat. So why do some teams get to the playoffs so often?

I believe the answer is that consistently successful teams have "football people" making football decisions. Generally, it's a tandem: a strong general manager and a good coach. They are usually people who have been in the game themselves. They don't get wrapped up in combine hype. "What's his forty time?" "Who cares! Can he separate and catch the ball?" They know how to draft, and they know how to trade for what they need. They can adapt a team's talent to an effective offense and defense, or change their schemes to fit the talent on hand.

Contrast these teams with those that have non-football people making key decisions. Sometimes the only qualification of the person selecting a draft choice is that he owns the team—or that his dad owns it. These teams have bad drafts, year after year. They make bad trades, and they fire a lot of coaches who otherwise might win if there was a long-term strategy.

I have some great and some not-so-great memories of the Seattle Seahawks' owners. In the beginning, Lloyd Nordstrom and his wife, Ilslay, were instrumental in getting an NFL franchise in Seattle. They brought together a group including Seattle businessmen Herman Sarkowsky, Howard Wright, Monte Bean, Ned Skinner, and members of the Nordstrom family to become the Seahawks' first owners. The team played its first season in 1976. Initially, Herman Sarkowsky was the managing partner, and later John Nordstrom. If anything, this group exemplified the attributes I associate with a successful team. They recognized that they had no experience in professional football, so they went out to find people who did. When they eventually became convinced that general manager John Thompson and coach Jack Patera couldn't get them to the next level, they went out and attempted to get even better people: Hall of Famer Mike McCormack and Chuck Knox.

The Nordstroms had deep roots in Seattle. They had been in the Pacific Northwest for generations. They had the kind of work, family, and business ethics that led to success. Publicly they were quiet and unassuming, generally operating in the background. There was no ostentatious display of wealth, no flash, no camera-seeking jigs on the sidelines. There was no boasting, no mouthing-off after a win over the Raiders or the Jets. There were no cutesy commercials and no boorishness. The Seahawks owners understood that there is no "I" in team—and that this maxim applies to owners, too. In the eight years that I worked with them, I have only fond memories of their gracious patience, loyalty, and respect for each man and the job he'd been chosen to do. They endured two strikes in which the players they'd invited into their homes for Christmas picketed and screamed epithets at them in front of their stores. In the end, they saw the NFL for what it was:

entertainment. It wasn't the Holy Grail. The Nordstroms eventually had to shift their time and resources as their company began a major expansion into California and the East Coast. They quietly tried to find a local buyer or to sell to one of the minority partners. No one from the Pacific Northwest could step up with the money. When a Californian became the front-runner, they decided to renegotiate their Kingdome lease into the year 2000 in an attempt to make it impossible for anyone to move the team elsewhere. This franchise had been their family's gift to the community of the Pacific Northwest, and before relinquishing control, they wanted to make sure it couldn't be spirited away. Only then, with much regret, did they sell the team to Ken Behring and a group of California investors.

The new owners' first major decision was to "find their own man," so they fired Mike McCormack. It appeared to be an ill-considered move. They didn't have anyone lined up to replace Mike. An interim general manager named Mike Blatt was brought up from California. Blatt's qualifications for this job seemed to be that he was the one who hooked the Nordstroms up with Ken Behring while he was negotiating on behalf of his client, quarterback Kelly Stouffer. He interviewed the medical staff in Mike McCormack's office. With his lizard-skin cowboy boots propped up on Mike's desk, he asked me if I'd be willing to shoot up a player's knee during a game if it would get that player on the field. When I indicated I would resign before doing something that stupid, he laughed nervously and said he was "just testing us." His body language gave me the creeps. Several weeks later, he was indicted for conspiracy to commit murder in a contract killing.

Ken Behring and his son David were always courteous and pleasant to me. I am grateful for their trust and for the opportunity they gave me to be the team doctor. Knowing them fairly well, I believe that they genuinely meant well and that they wanted to win. It just seemed to me that they were in way over their heads. In the press, the Seahawks were portrayed as Ken's new toy, one he didn't want to share. A host of factors doomed his relationship with Seattle. To begin with, he was a *California developer*. Uncontrolled growth was choking Seattle's highways and air with pollution. Washington's streams were silting up, and our salmon were disappearing. The cliché was, salmon can't spawn on asphalt. You can imagine how sympathetic the press was toward the Behrings. They were outsiders. In a more provincial community like ours, you needed to know your way around to get things done. They didn't.

Our first away game under Behring's ownership was a portent of things to come. We played the New York Jets, a team that, for inexplicable reasons, the Seahawks had always owned. Their talent, team record, injuries, or the score at halftime didn't matter—we just flat-out owned them. All that changed on national television in a rainstorm when the Jets kicked our ass. And then, instead of flying home with the team, the rich, absentee owners took their private jet. Were they too important to ride home with their own team? What happened to the sense of family? Also, there was a mystery woman riding home on the team plane. No one knew who she was, so rumors were rampant. Anything goes! In the coming months, things started to spin out of control. Seahawks defensive back Patrick Hunter wrecked his customized Mercedes. Running back Lamar Smith crashed the car he was driving in an accident that left Mike Fryar quadriplegic. Brian Blades accidentally shot his cousin to death in a brawl over a loaded gun. It was not uncommon to pick up the newspaper and see a story about someone claiming to have been assaulted by either a Seahawk coach or a player.

Our draft choices started to stink. We'd get a good one, and then some lemons. There was no consistency, top to bottom. We passed up Eric Mota (eventually San Diego's Pro-Bowl lineman), instead taking a wide receiver who he had blazing, 4.27 speed, but hadn't even started in college—and he couldn't catch the ball. Mike Allman sent one of us to Mississippi to carefully check out Bret Favre's hip. Mike had Favre graded at the top of his list. Sure, Dan McGwire was on the list, but lower. Dan was a California boy though, and that's who Behring wanted. Mike could barely suppress his frustration and anger. He slipped out of the draft war room. I passed him in the hall. "If they don't even listen to me," he muttered, "why are they paying me?" Eventually they fired Tom Flores, and then they solved Mike's problem by firing him as well. For reasons known only to Seahawk management, they waited until June, when all the NFL scouting jobs had been taken, before they brought down the axe on Mike Allman and Phil Neri. That mean-spirited action later cost the Seahawk management dearly in a grievance—full salary *and* attorney's fees.

Randy Mueller became the director of scouting. His football experience consisted of his time playing Division III football at Linfield College in Oregon. I don't mean to denigrate Randy. Essentially he was doing what everyone in the organization was trying to do: survive the capricious whims of a frustrated owner playing with his new toy. At that time, there wasn't a single person in management who had ever played a down in the NFL. The entire organization started to sink, and soon the franchise's very existence in Seattle was threatened.

In 1995, Art Modell pithed the collective psyche of the football world by moving Cleveland's beloved Browns to Baltimore. This was like cutting the heart out of the city or stoning your mother when she brings you a fresh-baked apple pie. He was cursed and vilified. Frequent death threats were made. John Bergfeld told me that the Cleveland Clinic, where the Browns got their medical care, received bomb threats. Modell's reasons for leaving Cleveland were quite simple: he was going bankrupt, and he wanted some money. Actually, he just kept spending money like all the other owners, and he expected the public to pick up the tab. Cleveland's intransigence and the convenient expiration of the Browns' stadium lease gave Modell the opening he needed. He got an immediate infusion of $50 million just by signing the Baltimore contract. A new stadium, luxury boxes, and an attractive concession package were also part of the deal.

This move set off a frenzy of lawyers churning billable hours as every NFL team searched for loopholes in their stadium and municipal contracts. Georgia Frontiere's Ram management determined that it was "just impossible" to make money in Los Angeles, thus triggering an escape clause in the Rams' contract that allowed the team to move to a lucrative new St. Louis stadium. Not surprisingly, the Raiders also escaped from Los Angeles amidst frantic bidding after proving that the LA Coliseum had not lived up to its contract promises. Tennessee was wooing the Oilers, prompting them to declare that, even though they had another year left on their Astrodome contract, as far as they were concerned, "they were gone." This announcement led to a surreal season in which a mere handful of Houston fans showed up to watch or boo the Oilers in the mostly empty stadium. The commissioner finally let the team slink out of town after they paid the city of Houston "damages" for the loss of the final season.

These events had visions of sugarplums dancing in the heads of some Seahawk owners. The newspapers were full of pictures of Ken Behring posing with Seagals and stories about his paying off a palimony lawsuit. This negative publicity did not endear him to the family-oriented Pacific Northwest. As development exploded across the state, laws and land regulations were enacted that cost Behring dearly in the Seattle market. It was rumored that he'd lost millions in attempted local real-estate deals. The previously sold-out Seahawks were now losing, and Mike McCormack, Chuck Knox, and Tom Flores had all been fired. There were few fans, and except for away games, the blackout rule for television was almost always in effect. The once full Kingdome was never sold out.

In 1996, as another losing season wound down, the Seahawks found themselves on the East Coast for an entire week. The team had played and beaten the Jacksonville Jaguars, but rather than fly home—only to fly back to D.C. for the Redskins—the team stayed out East. We practiced at a local Jacksonville high school football field. Art Modell had just turned the world of football on its ear, and the Browns' move was the hottest story on every sports channel. I was running laps around the practice field while the Seahawks drilled. David Behring sat in the stands and watched. Between laps we talked. I commented that it seemed to me that the owners had lost sight of the fact that the fans were the reason for the game, and that the owners were only stewards. I said I believed that if the owners weren't careful, they might destroy the game—kill the goose that was laying the golden eggs. David didn't seem very receptive to this notion, and his eyes sort of glazed over. I had once heard someone liken David to a little kid watching a freight train speeding by, filled with money. As teams moved and fortunes changed hands, he was frantically trying to figure out how he could jump on that train before it got past him.

Back in Seattle, a referendum to refurbish the Kingdome failed by only a half a percentage point. The Seahawk organization had studiously avoided all public comment on this referendum. It was speculated that the owners secretly hoped it would fail. When it did, they saw their opening. Behring's lawyers argued that the terms of the Seahawks' Kingdome contract—which required the Kingdome to maintain a first-class facility—had been breached. The Behrings used this as an excuse to try to escape to California. What followed was an organizational disgrace. The loyal people who had devoted their careers to the Seahawks never knew what hit them. Before announcing this move, the Behrings held a secret meeting. Coaches and selected staff were brought one by one into a conference room. They were informed that the team was moving to California, and they had to immediately decide whether they'd be willing to make the move. "Can I call my wife?" "No. Decide now. We'll make it worth your while." For most of the employees, that promise wasn't put into writing. For the coaches and staff, moving to California meant a huge pay cut. When you take into account the costs of moving and the housing costs in the inflated California real-estate market— not to mention the California income tax. For many in the organization who said yes, the "we'll make it worth your while" never happened. Jimmy told me about this meeting. He said it was like a surreal Spanish Inquisition. You were supposed to act happy, as if California was the coolest thing in the world. Never mind all the blood, sweat, and time the team had spent building goodwill in the Pacific Northwest community. That meant nothing.

The rest of the employees were fired. The Seahawk headquarters was closed, the locks were changed, and the phones were disconnected. Seahawk employees showed up for work, not realizing their jobs were gone, only to be turned away by newly hired guards. The moving vans came, and eventually everyone left. One week later, an embarrassed Mickey Loomis called me at the office. 'Oh, say, you guys are still going to the Indy combines for us, aren't you?"

Ken Behring held disingenuous press conferences in Los Angeles in which he crowed about "how good it was to be back in California." "Would the Coliseum, the Anaheim stadium, anyone, be interested?" As he trolled for deals, a leery California press published strongly negative sentiment. Then a legal salvo was fired from Washington state: Norm Maleng, the King County prosecutor, filed a lawsuit against the Seahawks *and* the NFL for breach of contract. Christine Gregoire, the state of Washington attorney general, filed a similar suit in federal court. Senator Slade Gordon suggested that perhaps the United States Senate might be interested in holding hearings on the antitrust exemption that the NFL enjoyed. As the heat got turned up, Commissioner Tagliabue finally had enough of this buffoonery. He informed the Behrings that if the Seahawks weren't immediately returned to Seattle to honor their Kingdome lease, they would be fined $50,000 per week until they did.

Community leaders headed by John Nordstrom formed a search committee to find a local buyer for the Seahawks. Even if the Behrings came back, it was obvious that they were so despised that the Seahawk franchise could never be successful. Under John's quiet leadership, Paul Allen was persuaded to step forward. Paul agreed to buy the Seahawks, but only if the people of the state of Washington wanted the team. Another referendum was held on a new, modernized stadium. If there were construction cost overruns, Paul Allen would cover them. This time, his organization campaigned for the issue. After a hard campaign, the referendum passed. Paul Allen, like the Nordstroms before him, appears to have the necessary, admirable ownership attributes. He's gone out and searched for the best people and then left them alone to do their jobs.

Coaches

Johnny Majors, Jackie Sherrill, Jack Patera, Chuck Knox, Tom Flores—these are some of the legendary head coaches with whom I've had the privilege of working. In 1976, the University of Pittsburgh won the NCAA national championship under Johnny Majors. His assistants included Jimmy Johnson, Jackie Sherrill, Dave Wannestedt, and Joe Avenzano. I remember back in 1977 when I was with the Panthers and we were in Syracuse, battling some fired-up Orangemen. It was a frigid Saturday afternoon on the sidelines, with billowing clouds racing overhead. We ran into the locker room at halftime. The score was close, but we were behind. In fact, if Syracuse hadn't turned the ball over twice during scoring drives, we'd have been getting killed. That afternoon, defensive line coach Jimmy Johnson gave one of the most inspirational halftime speeches I've ever heard. He absolutely blasted the D line, first humiliating them, then inspiring them, and finally igniting a seething rage that spilled out of the locker room and onto the field. I was practically looking for a helmet to strap on, myself! The D line charged out and annihilated Syracuse. Oh, I almost forgot to mention—Jimmy adjusted some line gaps and changed some blitzing schemes, too.

In my mind the hallmark traits of a great coach are the ability to use talent, to recognize schemes, to make adjustments on the run, and to inspire extra effort when none is left. In the NFL, the head coach is like the CEO of a corporation. Everything in the organization reflects his strengths, his ego, his drive to win, and his flaws. Each time the Seahawks hired a new head coach, it was like a psychic spasm that sent ripples through the entire organization. During my years with the Seahawks, we had four head coaches with completely different personalities: Jack Patera, Chuck Knox, Tom Flores, and Dennis Erickson.

Jack Patera

Jack Patera was the first head coach in the history of the Seahawk franchise. He was a huge, intimidating man, with a broad, ruddy face and penetrating dark eyes. But he also had a ready smile and a rumbling bass laugh. In his relations with the medical staff, he was always a gentleman. He was a close friend of my partner, Walter Krengel. Even after Patera was dismissed, they stayed fast friends. Injury reports were simple. "Who was hurt? Will they need surgery? How long will they be out?" Just like that. Not once did he try to second-guess us. He trusted us to take care of our responsibilities, and he'd take care of his. He was a gracious man who went out of his way to befriend me and to make me feel welcome in the organization. He also had an uncanny knack for making humorous, disarming comments that could defuse potentially explosive situations. One day, Efren Herrera, a very competitive kicker, made some emotional comments in a newspaper story, probably out of frustration with a loss. I don't remember exactly what the inflammatory remark was, but the press gleefully repeated it to Jack, expecting to ignite fireworks. But Jack just gave a deep laugh and smiled at the reporters. "Sounds like Efren ate a bad enchilada."

One of Jack's strengths also proved to be his undoing. Jack electrified Seattle with gimmick plays. You never knew what would happen on punts or special teams. On *Monday Night Football* in 1981, after Sherman Smith scored a touchdown on a fake field-goal attempt, Howard Cosell declared, "Jack Patera is giving the nation a lesson in football." Unfortunately, one can pull a rabbit out of a hat only so many times. For a while, Jack seemingly could make something out of nothing, season after season. But it takes years to build a solid offensive line, and as a 1976 expansion team, the Seahawks had no real offensive-line strength. Instead, we had young "projects" and a smattering of old line vets. Bad luck with injuries had also taken its toll. But it didn't matter, because our quarterback, Jim Zorn, was a scrambler. To counter a lack of protection for the quarterback, the offensive line used the "rolling pocket"—since our O line couldn't stop anyone, it would collapse in an orderly fashion. We perfected the "sprint draw" play, a counter play that allowed the O line to get beat but still provided a corridor for David Sims or Sherman Smith to run the draw. And we had the great Steve Largent.

As the years went by, we should have been accumulating talent. I was new to the organization, and I do not know the extent to which the managing partner did or did not interfere with the draft. But our drafts seemed like our plays—gimmicks. When I joined the Seahawks in 1980, Dick Mansberger was our chief scout. One of his claims to fame was scouting Calvin Hill, a running back from Yale, for the Dallas Cowboys. A running back from the Ivy League made it in the NFL? The football world was incredulous. Mansberger became the guru of the "overlooked gem." He specialized in finding hidden nuggets in the draft. "Never mind that this draft pick only played basketball in college—he's got great hands! He's projected at tight end!" Eventually, things started to unravel. In one draft, we traded up first-round picks and got Jacob Green. He turned out to be a brilliant choice, an All-Pro who played with us for 13 seasons. But we wasted a second-round pick on Andre Hines. Andre who? At Stanford he'd been a backup, not even a starter. Yet he was our second-round pick. A good team needs bread and butter with high draft picks, not gambles. Andre arrived at our Cheney training camp overweight and out of shape. Our internist said maybe his own wife was in better shape than Andre was. Andre liked hamburgers. Rather than admit defeat, it was decided that Andre would become a project. Andre spent his entire training camp trying to get into shape under the supervision of trainer Bruce Scott. He never made it.

At the same time we were wasting many high draft picks on gambles, some "old school" habits started to catch up with Jack. When he was an assistant coach under Bud Grant at Minnesota, there were no water breaks during two-a-day practices. Also, they allowed no gloves during the Minnesota winter. Maybe Bud believed that "real men" concentrated on football and didn't allow distractions such as heat stroke or freezing to death to interrupt practices. So Jack didn't permit water breaks at summer camp in Cheney. This practice was medically dangerous. Heat stroke in a 300-pounder is nothing to fool around with. After several years of trying to work around this problem, it became necessary for the team physicians to send a registered letter to the owners. The doctors disavowed all medical responsibility or liability should a heat event occur.

The undercurrent of these struggles in training camp, poor draft picks, and the gimmicks started to catch up with the team. People expected the Seahawks to win in 1981, but it was a losing season. Jack brought in a psychological "coach" named Johnny Kai. He was supposed to help the players "visualize winning." He had them sit in a vibrating electric chair in a room with the lights out. He spoke to them about things like life and death in the jungle. He told the trainers how a tape job should be counter-clockwise on a players' ankles to get the energy flowing "just right." Kai's flaky gimmicks destroyed any confidence the players might have had in the team's preparation. They'd scream a Johnny Kai karate "Keeeeeahhh!" and run out on the field. Then on the next play they'd get decked. We went 3–13. Jack released Kai.

The following year, the NFL Players Contract expired. Sam McCullough, the Seahawks' player rep, was a popular, well-liked receiver. In an effort to minimize the risks of player animosity during these contract negotiations, the owners gave specific orders that Sam should not be cut. In spite of this, Sam was released on the first cut-down. This action crystallized the animosity between the Seahawk players and reactionary management and the coach. The players went on strike. In the end, John Thompson and Jack Patera got the axe. Mike McCormack was hired as an interim coach and then accepted the general manager's job. These events ushered in a golden age under Chuck Knox.

Chuck Knox

Chuck Knox, old blue eyes, the General—what a wild ride we Seahawks had. Chuck Knox and his beautiful wife, Shirley, blew into town like a cool breeze after a long hot drought. He came via the Los Angeles Rams and Buffalo Bills. His intense eyes took in everything. He missed nothing. He was a winner. Preparation was his key: Know your team's strengths, know your enemy's weaknesses, disguise your moves, and play the percentages. Sun Tzu's *The Art of War* sat on his desk, the pages worn from reading. When Chuck held his first press conference as head coach of the Seahawks, he looked right at the camera with a piercing gaze. He announced that he intended to make the Seahawks competitive—immediately. He put on a royal blue Seahawk hat in workman-like fashion, grinned out at the press corps, and said, "Let's go kick some butt!"

And kick butt he did. We finished Chuck's first season winning a wild-card playoff spot. We beat Denver in Seattle in the first wild-card playoff game in Kingdome history. Then it was on to Miami and Dan Marino. The Dolphins had a fat-and-sassy 13–3 record, they were rested, and the East Coast press was already writing about who Miami would play after they had beaten us. Chuck adjusted the O-line's blocking splits, a move that caught Shula's defensive strategy off guard. We were ahead right up until the last five minutes when Dave Krieg missed a pass on a timing pattern. He threw the ball right into the arms of a stunned defender who then ecstatically ran it in for a Miami go-ahead touchdown. The Orange Bowl crowd went beserk with a deafening roar. Inside the two-minute warning, Largent screamed at Krieg above the noise. The Dolphins were crowding up on the line to stop Curt. Largent was in single coverage. Krieg connected with Largent on two bombs, and then Curt did an end-around on the right for the go-ahead touchdown. The Orange Bowl fell silent, but thousands of screaming fans met us at the Seattle airport at one o'clock that morning.

The Los Angeles Raiders ended this dream season in a dominating display of raw power and finesse for the AFC championship. There were brawls in the stands, a riot on the field, and multiple arrests as drunken, knife-waving bikers got rowdy. Herman Sarkowsky ran out at my side while I protectively wielded a steel medical case. Marcus Allen and company went on to win the Super Bowl. Al Davis said, "We take what we want." We went home to lick our wounds, wondering whether we lacked the talent to get to the next level, or whether we'd simply choked.

In 1983, his first year with the Seahawks, Chuck had made good on his promise to make us competitive. In 1984, Chuck Knox proved his coaching genius. Chuck's offensive orientation was centered around the weapon of running back Curt Warner. In Curt's rookie year, he was almost unstoppable, selected for both the All-Rookie Team and the Pro Bowl. So the following year in our opening game at the Kingdome against the Cleveland Browns, Chuck's offensive game plan was naturally to let Curt run wild—to destroy the opponent. In fact, Curt was unstoppable. Unstoppable, that is, until he blew out his knee. To replace him, Mike McCormack brought in Wilber Montgomery, but he flunked my physical with a bad knee. Next, they brought in Franco Harris, who had been holding out in a contract dispute with the Steelers. Unfortunately, it was soon apparent that Franco hadn't just lost a half step, he'd lost a yard! So Chuck threw out the team's offensive playbook and started over, adapting the Seahawks to the offensive skills that remained. We went 12–4 that year, made it back to the playoffs, and Chuck was voted AFC Coach of the Year.

With Mike McCormack at the managerial helm, Chuck kept the Seahawks in the playoff hunt virtually every year. When we won the AFC West title in 1988, we played the Bengals at Cincinnati in the playoffs. The Bengals' coach, Sam Wyche, had his own little gimmicky hurry-up offense, which amounted to nothing more than poor sportsmanship. He used a loophole in the rules, and it was trumpeted as smart coaching. The idea was, if the ball was spotted on the Bengals' side of the field, they'd huddle 13 or 14 players so that their opponent couldn't tell whether they intended to run or pass. If the opponent's defense brought in five defensive backs for pass defense, suddenly the Bengals would break out of the huddle and run to the ball. Meanwhile, their opponent would still be scrambling, trying to get the right defensive people on the field, but because they were on the far side of the field, the opponent couldn't get its players into position before the ball was snapped. Since the defense would have too many people on the field, Cincinnati could audible and throw a bomb, because they already knew the referees would call a penalty for "illegal procedure," too many defensive men on the field. If Cincinnati connected on the long pass, they could decline the penalty. If they missed, or if the ball was intercepted, they could get it back anyway by accepting the five-yard penalty. Chuck stopped this offensive charade in its tracks. Anytime Sam pulled his hurry-up shenanigans, Chuck had one of his players flop down on the field with an "injury." The referees were forced to call an injury timeout to get the player off the field. This injury timeout allowed the Seahawks to get the right defensive scheme on the field. This strategy drove the Bengals apoplectic.

With five minutes to go, Brian Blades actually caught the tying touchdown pass in the end zone. The instant replay showed it was a legal catch, but the referee who was behind Brian ruled that he had trapped the ball. Our defense stopped the Bengals' attack, and we ran a two-minute offense, but too little time remained, and the Bengals went on to the Super Bowl after defeating the Bills in the AFC championship. In the off-season, the League Rules Committee closed the loophole Wyche had exploited and "hurry-up" offense was banned. You could go with a no-huddle offense, but you no longer could substitute from the sidelines.

The fickleness of injuries and the trials of new ownership finally caught up with Chuck. In 1987, we won a supplemental lottery draft and picked up the much-hyped Butkus Award winner, linebacker Brian Bosworth. His personae and salary eventually caused tremendous dissension on the team. In 1988, All-Pro linebacker Fred Young demanded to be traded. Dave Krieg's erratic play never seemed to improve, and his maddening soap-dish fumbles finally led Chuck to trade Kenny Easley for a new quarterback, Kelly Stouffer. Ultimately, The Boz was a bust. Ken Behring bought the team, and the Seahawks went through one ineffective quarterback after another. Mike McCormack was sacked. Finally, so was Chuck. But Chuck Knox had shown the Seahawk organization and the community what it took to win. He was absolutely relentless in his attention to detail. He had street smarts, what he referred to as "Eighth Grade Sewickley," the common-sense things he learned about life while growing up on the steel-town streets of a Pittsburgh suburb. If he sensed for an instant that you were evasive or slacking off, you were gone. But he was forever loyal to those who worked hard and were loyal in return. I'll never forget one night in New Orleans when he took us all to dinner at an Italian restaurant. He knew the owner, so the restaurant was ours. We stayed out until two in the morning, singing at a piano bar. He brought out the best in all of us. His dedication in my copy of his book, *Hard Knox,* is signed, "To a great doctor and a good friend." Though I believe he was controversial in the end, Chuck Knox belongs in the Seahawks' Ring of Honor.

Tom Flores
The most gracious man who ever coached the Seahawks was Tom Flores. He was quiet, unassuming, and very loyal. His vivacious wife, Barbara, immediately immersed herself in our community. She brought the needed sense of family back to the organization even though the new California owners were regarded as outsiders. She made sure that all the Seahawk wives were recruited to organize fund-raisers for Children's Hospital. When the team had an away game, everyone went to Barbara's for lunch. If your wife was shy, tough luck! She got to sit next to Barbara so that everyone could meet her. If anyone ever associated the Flores with the hated Raiders, the association evaporated one millisecond after they met Barbara. Tom did the best that he could with what he had. He had a long-range plan that required

several years to implement. He also had an impatient, meddling owner. It was a dysfunctional disaster. First, we went from one quarterback bust to the next. Tom inherited Kelly Stouffer, then tried big old slow Dan McGwire (bless his heart), and finally Rick Mirer.

Joe Vitt left with Chuck Knox, so Tom hired a new conditioning coach who had a track background. Soon, all the players were either running their butts off in gassers or sitting on the sidelines, nursing pulled muscles and tendonitis. As the year went by, I noticed Chinese herbs, caffeine pills, and deer-antler powder starting to reappear in the training room—shades of Johnny Kai. When players start getting their asses kicked, they'll reach for any gimmick, any magic solution, anything to win. Injuries were rampant. It is a well-known sports axiom that in collisions, the "hittee" has a much greater chance of injury than the "hitter," and we were getting hit plenty. At one time, we had more than 29 players on injured reserve. The players were being conditioned for track, not for football.

We members of the medical staff tried to warn Tom that something was wrong, that in the history of the franchise, we had never seen so many injuries. Tom showed great loyalty to his coaching staff, and in the end, I believe that loyalty—his refusal to make needed personnel changes—cost him his job. Here was a gracious man with four Super Bowl rings and two decades of NFL experience. You'd think the owners might have been more patient. I wish Tom could have had a chance to finish what he started.

Dennis Erickson

"This is the man we've wanted all along, Pierce. This man is a winner." I was being introduced to Dennis Erickson. I reached out to shake his hand. He wouldn't meet my eyes, glancing evasively at the floor. I was stunned, but I'd seen all kinds of mystifying behavior in people, so I decided not to fret too much about it. After all, Al Davis, Joe Gibbs, Jimmy Johnson, and Bill Parcells were each quite different, and yet each of them wore what we all coveted, a Super Bowl ring. Dennis's eccentricity may have seemed weird to me, but Dennis was a winner, wasn't he?

He wasn't. The first real clue that there was something wrong came after we gave Dennis the medical assessment of the potential draft choices following combine physicals. It takes a couple of hours to go over who failed his physical, who didn't, and the hated threes. The importance of this exercise is obvious. Jimmy told me that as they left the room, Dennis told him that going over medical grades was the biggest waste of time he'd ever seen.

As our first season under Dennis progressed, the situation got worse. Dennis tried to institute a "no practice, no play" rule. Such a rule might be okay in college, when you're four deep on the depth chart at every position with a 120-man roster. But in the NFL, sometimes you need to rest a ball player's hip pointer or cracked ribs. With judicious injection of Marcaine before the kickoff and a "flak jacket" or hip pad for protection, the team could be at full strength for a game. But Dennis had his rules, and the trainers suffered a constant berating for not having the squad at full strength on the practice field.

I was never sure that Dennis ever understood injuries. For example, injury reports on Monday morning after the Sunday game were absolutely critical. If you didn't know who was hurt and for how long, how could you plan strategy? It's hard to believe the following conversation actually took place, but it did. I gave Dennis the injury report.

"Coach, Terry has a pulled hamstring. He'll be out three weeks at least, maybe as long as six."

"Ah, what's that mean?"

Dennis also threw tantrums in the locker room. Before Monday morning injury clinics, the trainers were frequently berated in front of the players for not getting the players back onto the field *even before they'd seen the trainers to have their injuries diagnosed.* Soon the assistant coaches joined this pecking party—at least there was someone else to blame for losing beside themselves. One assistant coach was quoted in the press bad-mouthing the care the Seahawks got. "You never know what's going to happen to our players when they go into that training room." He was fined and told to shut his mouth. After several years of coaches casting doubt on our trainers, injured players started leaving camp to get treated.

In a 1997 game in Baltimore against the Ravens, Winston "Dirt" Moss and Chad Brown did an end-around blitz on the quarterback. Testaverde ducked, and the two linebackers collided, helmet to helmet, just like in the New York Jets Dennis Byrd incident. Chad lay stunned on the ground with a severe concussion. Somehow, Dirt got up on his own and got off the field. The adrenaline was still flowing, and he actually went back out for one more play. Then he took himself out of the game. He could feel that something was wrong. The X rays in the locker room weren't satisfactory, so my partner sent Dirt to the hospital for better films and a CAT scan. Jimmy told me that at halftime, a coach started berating the players. "Don't go near the trainers or doctors; they'll take you out of the game." It turned out that Dirt had a broken neck. One wrong move could have left him quadriplegic or dead. It would require months in halo fixation to heal the fracture. Chad's concussion didn't clear until the fourth week. At the end of that season, Winston Moss retired. At the end of the next season, the staff, coaches, and doctors were asked to sign a gag clause prohibiting them from discussing any aspect of the team without the expressed permission of management. Fortunately, since I had already stepped down, this didn't apply to me.

The Seahawk organization and Winston Moss owe Kevin Auld a huge debt for his persistence and wisdom. Part of me wants to follow the principles of the Walt Disney movie *Bambi* in which Thumper says, "If you don't have nothin' nice to say, don't say nothin' at all." But another part of me is glad that Dennis is gone and wishes he'd never been in Seattle. In four years, Dennis Erickson wiped out 20 years of goodwill and the perception that our medical staff was one of the finest in the NFL. The contagion of his stain spread to the trainers. When Mike Holgrem took over, he asked the players what they thought of the trainers. After four years of losing under Dennis, the players didn't trust anyone. In the end, both Jimmy and Todd were let go. For 23 years, Jimmy had given his heart and soul to the Seahawks. In another hundred years, the organization may never have another trainer of his caliber: NFL Trainer of the Year, Trainer's Hall of Fame. The Seahawk organization didn't even give him a good-bye banquet. He deserves better. Like Chuck Knox, he deserves to be in the team's Ring of Honor.

Agents

When the movie *Jerry Maguire* came out, every sports agent in America sat smugly in the theater and said, "Yeah, that's what I'm all about." Would that they were all so noble! The movie also resulted in a giant headache for existing NFL agents, because now a lot of wannabes tried to become agents! The 1998 NBA strike illustrated the power of today's elite agents. When a bitter NBA management team couldn't reach a collective bargaining agreement with the players, they claimed that the agents of veteran players, not the negotiating team, were actually calling the shots in the strike. Agents are now part of multiple-division corporations that have trust divisions, real-estate divisions, equity investment insurance, and labor divisions. When contracts start rolling out $10-million signing bonuses on a routine basis, we're talking big money. The agent gets a small piece, between two and three percent, not counting "finder's fees" they may collect from investments.

I talked about the changes in agenting with Jack Mills of Boulder, Colorado. Jack has been an agent representing NFL players for over 32 years. He represents approximately 35 active NFL players, from rookie free agents with minimum salaries to stars with $26-million-dollar contracts. I asked him to summarize the biggest difference between then (the good old days) and now. He writes, "The biggest difference today is the heavy recruiting of prospective clients and the offering of marketing incentives or guarantees to potentially high draft clients. There are simply so *many* more agents today, many of whom have no clients or only one or two who are on an active roster in the NFL. There is a lot of illegal recruiting. One agent was arrested in Seattle during the old combine days, procuring prostitutes for potential players. Rules have been set up regarding agent behavior, but unless the NFL Players Association enforces the rules and regulations, they mean nothing.

"The second biggest change for agents was the introduction of free agency for the players with four or more years, and the salary cap. The salary cap, with its many technical features and schemes, made negotiating contracts much more complex." It's so complex, Mills said, that most agents now carry their own professional liability or "malpractice" insurance. A player getting bad advice or a bad contract won't hesitate to sue his agent.

I also asked Jack about injuries to his clients. He believes it is now a standard practice in the NFL to get a second, outside opinion. It might prick the balloon of the ego of the team physician, but it simply makes sense now that medicine has become so complex. In his own practice, he frequently contacts the team physician himself to hear the doctor's perspective on the player's injury. He also believes that some teams will release a hurt scrub who has no chance to make the team, believing that the player is too dumb to realize what has happened. But if the player happens to be a savvy veteran, they will try to make an injury settlement. If that hurt player fills a grievance, that action ties up salary-cap money until the grievance is settled. This can financially handcuff the team from a cap standpoint, and they can still wind up losing the grievance. In Jack Mills's opinion, it makes better business sense to work out an injury settlement.

Mike McCormack told me that he believes that the very first football agent represented a player with the Green Bay Packers during the Vince Lombardi era. When that player notified Green Bay management that an agent would be negotiating his next contract, the player was promptly released. Mike told me this after he'd negotiated Steve Largent's last contract. Steve was a dinosaur—he represented himself.

In the past, an agent would negotiate what he believed represented fair market value for his client-athlete and take out a percentage for himself. In the NBA, under the rookie salary cap, agents generally negotiate that first contract for free, because the rookie contracts are already set, structured under the NBA's new collective bargaining agreement. There is no real function for an agent at this time. The goal of the agent is to ingratiate himself with the player, giving him investment tips and financial planning advice, in an effort to get the player to agree to allow him to negotiate the *second* contract. In the NFL, the days of a simple contract are gone, and the agents are much more important. Today, a new contract might include a scholarship fund in the athlete's name for his college or university. It also includes homes and cars for his immediate family. How about access to a luxury box for the player's family and friends? Then there's money management: annuities, deferred income, tax-free income, guaranteed income, bonuses, roster bonuses, performance bonuses, reporting bonuses, severance clauses, and injury protection.

The agents are governed by rules of conduct. An agent found illegally recruiting clients or mismanaging money can be barred by the players association. Access to player-clients is crucial. The NFL Players Association and the agents hammered out an agreement on agent behavior, and an agent who violates the agreement can be suspended. Once upon a time, the League itself could also drive an agent out. Maybe it still can. There was no paper trail. Management from each of the clubs would tell the top prospects well before the draft that if they wanted to be considered high in the draft, they should consider the following list of agents to represent them. An agent who was abrasive and encouraged his clients to hold out didn't appear on the list. Pretty soon, that guy was gone. It will be interesting to see if Joey Galloway's agent is still representing football players in the future or if he'll suddenly find himself without clients.

Control is power. One subtle change that occurred over the years is that the agents have convinced football players that the agents, and only the agents, care about their welfare. Everyone else is suspect: team management, the NFL drug testing officer, the trainer, and even the doctor. Maybe they're not necessarily enemies; they just don't have the player's welfare close to their heart—not like his agent does. When I entered the league in 1980, I can't recall a player ever leaving his team to get care elsewhere. As Jack Mills pointed out, nowadays a second opinion is almost standard. It's common for a football player to have surgery performed by someone other than his team's doctor. This change came about for a variety of reasons. For one thing, there is a broad discrepancy among teams in the quality of care provided. In my 20 years of practice, a wave of technological advances has swept the field of orthopedics. For example, in 1971, we surgeons were taught that a torn anterior cruciate ligament was an inconsequential injury. Early attempts at surgical repair were failures. As we learned more, our profession decided we needed to better understand how this ligament functioned. So we tried to fix the ligament, and we still did a pretty poor job of it. These surgeries were huge, mutilating operations. Then the arthroscope came along, and suddenly the whole procedure could be done swiftly, effectively, and with high rates of success. However, there were a lot of "old school" doctors out there who didn't keep up. This led agents, naturally, to look around for the best care.

The second reason that loyalty to a team's medical staff disappeared came with the last NFL Players Collective Bargaining Agreement. Free agency arrived. Talented players could move from one team to another, and any sense of team loyalty or "family" tended to evaporate. A rich free agent who got hurt was essentially on a team of strangers. How could he really know whether the team doctor was any good or not? He could only trust that his agent would look out for his interests. For a young new agent, this added an extra power trip, an opportunity to demonstrate to the club how important he was. Control is power. When Curt Warner blew out his knee in 1984, his agent, Marvin Demoff, asked us if we could call and let him know how things went. In 1998, a backup Seahawk free-agent defensive back was hustled out of camp for a metatarsal fracture that almost any first-year orthopedic resident could have fixed. The reality was, the agent wanted to send the team and his player a message: I have control. The player thought it was really cool that the agent cared so much about him. In fact, the player didn't realize that the agent was using him as a bargaining tool to send a message to the club.

A third reason that agents insist on outside surgery for their players is that many clubs have, in effect, neutered their team physicians. Injuries are the one thing that coaches can't control, and they drive control-freak coaches crazy. Coaches hate it when the doctor tells them that a star player will be out for four to eight weeks, maybe more. The solution to this maddening intrusion? Remove the doctor from the team. The doctors are intentionally excluded from team activities. They have to eat separately, they can't ride to the game on the team bus, and the coach will take the injury report from the trainer only. In other words, for a player who is wondering whether he can play hurt or not, the control-freak coaches want the player to ask *them* that question, not the doctor. The conventional doctor–patient relationship is nonexistent, and the trust naturally fostered by such a relationship is consciously undermined by the organization. This puts the team physician at greater risk for malpractice.

On the flip side are those physicians who curry the agents' favor. They fly agents and players around in private jets. They maintain condos for the agents. They have their own public-relations people. Do these doctors have conflicts of interest? Many of these "experts" have a whole slew of sports-medicine fellows running around, just drooling for another case. How many operations are ghosted? Every time one of those doctors holds a press conference announcing how he just saved someone's career, the player needs to ask himself, "Did *he* really do the surgery?" Keep in mind, some of these so-called medical experts have been corresponding with their state disciplinary boards, and some who trumpet their expertise may not even be board certified. Beware, beware!

Every year someone wins the Super Bowl, but the idea of building a team through the draft, of having a sense of loyalty and family as the team grows and wins, is gone. Owners try to buy Super Bowls through free agency, just as some teams in baseball have bought the World Series. In this climate, agents will continue to be a force to be reckoned with.

I believe that in the future, the NFL's greatest challenge will be to recognize when it has reached its financial limit. In fact, I believe it already has. Our country has been through an unprecedented, two-decade period of economic expansion. Fabulous wealth has been created. However, 50 million baby boomers are now peering hesitantly past middle age and down the road toward the certainty of their own mortality. These are the people who have created the new wealth of this country. In the past, they have supported sports, but I believe that now they're turning away from sports fanaticism as they begin to think about more important life goals. *Monday Night Football* is no longer a religion. In fact, only with careful market tinkering (the best teams, the best television markets, cutesy computer-generated graphics and comedians) has it survived at all. The collective yawn when the NBA went on strike in 1998 provided ample evidence of this baby-boomer apathy. Who cared? To survive, the NFL must stay in touch with its fan base. For those who like sports—the coal miner, the steelworker, the car salesman, and maybe even the geek who programs a computer—luxury boxes have no relevance.

The league will need to remain affordable and continue to reinvent itself. I believe professional sports as a whole has tapped out its fan base. They've pushed the envelope as far as it will go. When the next economic downturn comes—and it will—unemployment will increase and corporations will downsize. Luxury boxes will be vacant. Shareholders will start screaming about the cut in dividends while their money is being wasted on the advertising rights to the RCA Dome or Safeco Field. The world of pro sports will have to kiss the perks good-bye. At the same time, state governments and municipalities will continue to balk at referendums for new half-billion-dollar stadiums with luxury boxes. The blackmail of "build it or we'll move" will become an empty threat. Generation X has become the Now Generation. They don't have the time or inclination to waste an entire day at a sports event. Technological change will make it possible for them to watch the game on a handheld portable computer or download it for later, edited for commercials. As Los Angeles did when the Raiders left, the public of tomorrow will say, "So what?" The baby boomers will be watching their own grandkids play midget-league football. It's more fun, truly amateur, and free. So for the league, the players association, and the agents, the challenge will be to stay in touch with reality, to know when it's time to stop squeezing their fan base for more money.

Anyone who reads this book and concludes I left the NFL with some bitterness didn't really read the book! Sure, I've seen some genuinely nice people treated poorly by slobs who hide behind their power and wealth. Welcome to the real world! The trainers and some of the doctors who got the shaft are still loved and respected throughout the nation for what they did. Those other guys in the owner's luxury boxes? Who cares! For me, these past two decades in medicine have been a labor of love. Sports medicine has been one of the greatest, most rewarding careers I could ever imagine. When I started, I was one of only 28 NFL team physicians in the world. For 17 years, I was able to make a significant positive impact in the lives of many young athletes. I made friends for life with other doctors around the country from our encounters on the field of battle. I saw the world and grew professionally.

Furthermore, I witnessed and participated in a great health-care revolution. Our efforts to meet the needs of elite athletes translated into a quantum improvement for the care of everyday people. Think about it: When I started, our profession didn't even understand the anterior cruciate ligament, let alone know how to fix it. Gale Sayers and God-only-knows how many other aspiring athletes saw their dreams end with a painful twist and a pop. They now had a "trick knee"—the trick being how to understand what the heck was going on! Our first attempts at surgery were clumsy and involved huge, mutilating operations that required a year or more of rehabilitation. Now, a 35-minute arthroscopic outpatient procedure can give a 58-year-old woman the ability to play recreational tennis again or a 65-year-old man the chance to ski again. Such advances came about because we refused to give up on someone else's dream. Ask your managed care plan about that!

Eventually, because I'm also a baby boomer, I came to see that football is just entertainment, only a game. When I open the entertainment section of the newspaper, sometimes I see a movie I'd like to see, and sometimes I don't. That's what happened for me one day with the NFL. I suddenly lost interest in one form of Sunday entertainment. I've been blessed with a great wife and two wonderful sons. There's also a lot of deep powder to ski through, a lot of dry mayflies to present to unwary rainbow trout. It's time for me to step out of my partner's way and let him have his own experiences. The medical care of the Seattle Seahawks remains in great hands.

INDEX